For all people struggling with inflammatory bowel diseases (IBD), colon cancer, and ostomies, hope is all around you. And for the loved ones and caregivers that support those dealing with IBD, cancer, and ostomy, your love, care, and attention has been a precious gift, and we thank you.

Contents

Foreword . . . . *vii*

Acknowledgements . . . . *xi*

Introduction *1*

To Begin *3*

A-E *13*

F-J *37*

K-O *60*

P-T *79*

U-Z *113*

To Conclude *129*

What's Your Story? *133*

Appendix A, The Role of the Intestine *135*

Appendix B, What is Crohn's Disease? *136*

What Causes Crohn's Disease and
Ulcerative Colitis? *137*

How Common is IBD
(Inflammatory bowel disease)? *137*

Who Gets IBD? *138*

What is Ulcerative Colitis? *139*

Appendix C, Colorectal Cancer *140*

Appendix D, The Various Types of Ostomies *142*

Appendix E, Informational Websites *145*

About the Author *147*

Foreword

by Joy Boarini

C hoices. We are faced with hundreds of them every day. Some choices we make are easy while some are hard or even agonizing. Consequences of those choices may be immediate while others may take longer to recognize their effect on our lives. The choice to specialize in ostomy care as a WOC (Wound, Ostomy, Continent) Nurse was an easy choice for me and one that has had a significant impact on my career as a nurse.

It started when I heard, "Uncle Ed has cancer and is going to have an ostomy." As the only nurse in the family at the time, I realized that I needed to brush up on my knowledge and skills of stoma care. The last time I remembered caring for an ostomy patient was in nursing school when Sister Elizabeth helped me teach a patient how to irrigate their colostomy.

In my search for information, I met a nurse in our medical center that actually *specialized* in ostomy care. Millie gave me some booklets to read, and I quickly realized that there was a lot more to know. Millie offered to let me make rounds with her as she took care of ostomy patients all day long.

I expected to study the technical skills from Millie that day, but I received much more. I learned it was not just about recovering from the surgery and having a pouch. It was about compassion, education, family involvement, adjustments, coordination of care, creativity, and the problem solving skills needed when a pouching system doesn't work.

Another choice followed and soon afterward, I left for Emory University to specialize in this aspect of nursing. A few years later, my family made a choice to move to Minnesota where I met Bonnie Sue Rolstad. Together, we shared our passion for education and ostomy care and started a nursing specialty program at Abbott Northwestern Hospital.

Years later, another choice led me to accept a job at Hollister Incorporated with my career still focused on education. I use my specialized nursing knowledge and experiences daily as I speak with nurses, families, and people with ostomies.

Surprisingly, today there are still a great number of people with ostomies that are underserved. They may deal with technical problems with their ostomy or skin issues that are overwhelming. They may lack knowledge about how to move forward in their lives after having ostomy surgery. They may not know who to talk to because they have not been back to see their ostomy nurse for more than ten years. Some may have to make the choice between buying the correct ostomy supplies or food and some make a choice to reach out for help.

Recently I spoke with a thirty-year-old man on the phone. He said he had seen a nurse specialist in the hospital where he had his ostomy surgery. Although he acknowledged she knew what she was doing, he said she seemed overwhelmed and unhappy. That made an impact on him and me. As nurses, we all know it is not only *what* we do but *how* we do it that can make a difference. This man was savvy enough to seek out other sources of education and inspiration. Sadly, some people never do.

Some of this is the result of changes in our health care delivery system. These health care changes have been dramatic whether you are a consumer or a provider. Hospital stays are days instead of weeks. The insurance maze is confusing and difficult to maneuver. There is a shortage of nurses and the hours are long and the demands many. Nurses who are not specialized in ostomy care have become increasingly important.

As nurses, each patient we care for deserves the best we have to give whether we are in an ICU, extended care facility, or a person's home. Each one of us can make a difference for the person with an ostomy. We can make the choice to help them feel "normal" by providing a caring touch, asking enough questions, giving them educational booklets, or making a referral to a WOC nurse.

We do need more WOC nurses but every nurse needs to make an effort to improve their knowledge about ostomy care. Procedures and products have evolved and technologies have advanced. We must continue our education, read, attend conferences, support meetings, and listen to our patients while making a conscious choice to think of how our actions, our facial expressions, and our comments impact the lives of the ostomy patients we encounter.

During presentations on ostomy care, nurses in my audience will often comment about the fact that I remember the names and circumstances of each case discussed. Although the stomas or skin problems presented were interesting from a clinical perspective, to me they are people—real people with families, with names, with individual stories. Stories that make me cry, make me laugh, and make me care.

I am moved by the stories Brenda has included in this book. Many of the stories involve people who have made courageous choices. In the face of difficult and terrible diagnoses, they made the choice to move forward. Later, with their ostomy, they tell stories of living not compromising. They share wonderful examples of using laughter as part of their healing process. Their choices affected their lives and those around them.

In thinking of the many families of people living with ostomies, the word "we" gets used a lot. "We" had our ostomy last fall, "we" went through chemotherapy after the surgery, or "we" have gone back to work. They may not be conscious of the fact they say "we" but they made a choice to be involved and supportive of their loved one. If you are a family member or friend of someone with an ostomy, you, too, will find that you are a part of the humor and inspiration shared in this book.

I am glad you chose to pick up this book, and I know you will be inspired by what you read. We never know where our choices may lead us!

—*Joy Boarini, MSN, WOC nurse is an author, national speaker, wife, and mother. She is a manager in Clinical Education and Professional Service for Hollister Incorporated.*

Acknowledgements

Thanks to all those who contributed stories. I appreciated getting to know you. Thanks to Hollister Incorporated for your vision and your commitment to people living with ostomies around the globe. Thanks to my sisters, Laurie, Shelly, Amy, Cathy, Chris, and Kim, for reading, correcting, and honest opinions. Thanks to Rosemarie Dakota for help with organizing papers. Thanks to Sharron and Harry Stockhausen at Expert Publishing, Inc. and Jay Monroe at Mori's Studio. Thanks to my dear friends Sherry and Doug Wenborg for lending me their cabin for uninterrupted days. Thanks to Monica Sausen, Renee Rongen, and my Mom and Dad who were my sounding boards. A special thanks to my family, Bahgat, John, and Jehan for understanding energy constraints and necessary time alone. I am blessed to be surrounded by such goodness in my life.

Introduction

A few years ago when I wrote my first book, *If the Battle is Over, Why am I Still in Uniform?*, I wanted to get it into the hands of my fellow ostomates (people who have had alternative surgery for bodily functions) at the United Ostomy Association's national conference. I turned to the manufacturer of products I wear, Hollister Incorporated, and asked them to provide a book for each person at the conference. They agreed because they liked the honesty and the ordinary of my book.

Shortly after, they provided an opportunity for me to speak across the country to nurses and others who work with people living with ostomies. I began a whirlwind tour of twenty cities in ten weeks across the United States giving talks about humor and healing from the patient's viewpoint. Many health professionals appreciated the inside scoop on what the patient goes through after a diagnosis that requires an ostomy.

The quality work that our medical people do in attending to our ostomy concerns helps us to recover quickly to enjoy our lives once again. We look forward to the day when we will complain about taking out the trash, doing our homework, or even the tedious task of cleaning out the refrigerator. Ultimately, we hope to return to a life filled with better health and happiness.

One of the highlights of my travels took me to Hollister's manufacturing plant in Stuarts Draft, Virginia, where they produce my pouch. It humbled me to think about people working hard each day to make my life more manageable. Like many, I'm sure they would rather be shopping, fishing, or playing with their children; instead, they put in their shift at the plant, paying close attention to detail. They make a product that makes me feel secure, allows me comfort, and helps me to put my health concerns behind me.

Meeting the people at the plant gave me a bigger perspective on the many ways our society is integrated. I have a health problem, I get a medical diagnosis, and after much testing, I have surgery. By this time, probably over two hundred people were connected to me in some vital way, directly or indirectly. From billing to blood work to pathology to housekeeping to reception to filing paperwork. The technicians, the medical staff, the janitorial staff, the mailing people, the computer people, the cafeteria workers, and the parking lot attendants all play a role in my health care.

My horizons of care expand as I understand how people in international offices and production plants here and abroad are intertwined. Their efforts assure my confidence in their quality products. Indirectly, each associate in ostomy care has had an impact on my life. An estimated 700,000 ostomates live in North America. Hollister provides health care to over ninety countries and six continents affecting the health and well-being of millions of people. If I was traveling in Australia and left my supplies on the plane that just took off, I could find replacements available.

The research and development teams, along with the expert nurses on staff, play an important role in patient care. They improve ostomy products by finding solutions to challenges presented by the patients and their nurses, benefiting all of us living with an ostomy.

Out of my personal experience and many shared stories with health professionals, ostomates, and their loved ones, I am happy to bring you *I'd Like to Buy a Bowel Please*.

To Begin

I'm guessing if you picked up this book, you have a wacky sense of humor, are obsessed with bowels or a lack of bowels, are an ostomate, or perhaps love or care for someone living with an ostomy. I hope reading the experiences of others helps you in some way.

It can take guts to read a book like this. Actually, scratch that. You don't really need a lot of guts to read this at all. I found out, and so will you, that you can survive beautifully, do amazing things, and have a great sense of humor with less guts than you can imagine.

I'd Like to Buy a Bowel Please came about because there needed to be a place where people could express another angle about what it is like to deal with an ostomy. (Ostomy is the term when talking about colostomy, ileostomy, or urostomy.) I am an ostomate (a person living with an ostomy), and I asked people to share a funny story relating to their ostomies. I wanted to show that people could reach a place in their lives where they could laugh about dealing with their ostomy instead of crying or totally falling apart. Some people found inner strength from overcoming such a health obstacle, and they provided an inspirational message from their unique perspective. Other stories are just a slice of ordinary life with perhaps a little glitch thrown in.

Why should we find humor in the midst of dealing with ulcerative colitis, Crohn's Disease, or colon cancer? Is it possible to laugh at a person's intimate story dealing with their ostomy? It might seem sacrilegious to express amusement at a problem that can cause anxiety in which you fear you won't escape the house again, but it is possible to get over the devastation and laugh at yourself. Many of us felt in the beginning that life would never be routine again. Instead, for many IBD (inflammatory bowel disease) sufferers, life became normal for the first time in years because of surgery. The immediate search for a bathroom when they entered a shopping mall or party was over. When plagued by inflammatory bowel disease, a person's life can seem severely limited. Ostomates relayed they always carried a change of clothes, knew the route to the nearest restrooms on the way to school or work, and were afraid to travel by car or plane for fear of having an accident. Ironically, after surgery, they were able to enjoy their lives more fully-capable of doing just about anything they wished to do.

I am not suggesting that everyone run out to the colon and rectal surgeons to line up for ostomy surgery. New medications to manage the debilitating episodes of IBD or effects of colon cancer are being researched, and we continue to hope for a cure. The two bouts I had with abdominal cramps similar to those described by others was more than I would wish on anyone. Much worse than childbirth, on both occasions I feared I would die; the pain was so intense. Some of the people in these stories dealt with that kind of pain for days, months—even years. With guidance from their physician, individuals must weigh ostomy surgery as an option.

In the process of writing this book, I encountered only one person who was angry at the thought of anyone being able to laugh at such a dire predicament. He was not adjusting well to having an ostomy and had too many problems to feel optimistic about his days ahead. It can be extremely overwhelming to have poop flying out of your abdomen when you least expect it. In the early days with an ostomy, things may not go smoothly. It's not a natural event for most people and it can be extremely unsettling. People learn to cope because they want to move ahead in their lives the best they can.

I share some of my trials in my first book, *If the Battle is Over, Why Am I Still in Uniform?* In 1995, at the age of thirty-nine, I went to the doctor expecting to schedule hemorrhoid surgery; instead, I found out I had carcinoma of the rectum. Cancer is an equal opportunity mutant cell. It will let itself appear anywhere on the body. My private situation became very public in a matter of hours. I had a huge family, a thriving small business, and many connections in the community. Within minutes, there were phone calls made organizing prayer chains and offering help. Part of me thought it seemed a more reasonable approach to handle this colorectal cancer episode of my life in a very private manner. Who wants to talk about their bowels? It would mean sharing intimate details about a part of my body that was not a popular subject, certainly not worthy of dinner conversation in most households. The other part of me was so horrified at the thought of not surviving, I felt my loved ones were my only lifelines, and I clung the best I could. I would soon find out how a golf ball-sized tumor had wreaked havoc on my body.

Hours after leaving the clinic and surrounded by family, my aunt asked me, "Do you have colon cancer, cancer of the rectum, or colorectal cancer?" Unsure at the time, I guessed correctly that in this case, they were all the same since I learned at the doctors' office that the rectum is the lowest part of the colon. I felt that colon cancer was the "pretty" term for colorectal cancer. Somehow, "colon" sounded gentler and less threatening than colorectal cancer.

For many people there are few symptoms before colon cancer is detected, making the need for an ostomy quite a shock. My body-altering surgery would be a small price to pay for prolonging my life. My children were three and five years old at the time of my surgery. I wanted that cancer out of my body; I had no regrets or second thoughts.

My husband and I waited for test results with our anxious family and friends. We shared news from the doctor about my need to have extensive surgery in order to survive, including having a permanent colostomy, which, according to the doctor, was the good news. That kind of good news is like the dentist telling you that you only needed two root canals and four crowns instead of seven, or the fire department telling you that your house has burned down but your garage is still standing. The doctor cautioned me that if the cancer had spread to my liver or lungs, he would not perform the operation. Instead, they would make me as comfortable as possible. Then the gravity of the situation really hit me. A colostomy was sounding better all the time. Forget the idea of a luxurious tummy tuck and optional breast lift; bring on the colostomy.

A clean CAT scan and chest x-ray would lead the way for positive news. From what they could tell, it appeared the tumor was located entirely in the rectum and had not spread anywhere else. Even though my rectum would have to be removed, my cheeks sewn shut, part of my vagina reconstructed, a complete hysterectomy done, and I'd be pooping into a "bag" the rest of my life, I would *have* a life. I would live.

The constant support seemed to lessen the stress, knowing that so many people cared about me and my family. They cooked us meals, cleaned our house, or shared time with us. My husband enjoyed receiving the meals so much, I could just imagine I'd be saying, "Come on honey, it's been ten years. Don't you think I should ask the church ladies to stop?" There are benefits that come with facing a life threatening illness, and food was a bonus for my husband.

I was vocal about what I was going through in coping with my ostomy or maybe I just couldn't stop myself. First, I had to explain to my loved ones what having an ostomy was like. With some friends and family, I even did a little show-and-tell so they could better understand. Perhaps the steady stream of morphine reduced my inhibitions because I was not shy. Most people, myself included, had never encountered anyone dealing with an ostomy. In the beginning, it was obsessive conversation, obsessive thoughts, obsessive worries about smells, and a preoccupation with health and longevity—and rightly so.

I had physical problems keeping the pouch on and often my humor was on the sarcastic side. As time went by and I learned to live with the challenges of my colostomy, my true wit reappeared, which brought out the humor in others too.

These days, one of the best compliments I get is when a family member or friend forgets I have an ostomy. I look normal again—I am; it is just a new kind of normal. Initially, when many of us found out we would need surgery resulting in an ostomy, we could only react with disgust at the idea. Having stool or urine go into a bag (or the newer name of pouch) attached to our bodies the rest of our lives is an overwhelming reality. Some people have been sick for so long, an ostomy was perhaps their last chance at life, and they would reluctantly agree to surgery—only after trying everything else, which included years of medications and dietary restrictions.

There are many reasons why people end up with ostomies besides the bowel diseases mentioned earlier. I have met people who were born with their intestines and internal organs on the outside of their bodies and never had more than a day when they didn't have an ostomy, sometimes even requiring two because of the need for a place for urine as well as stool output. Others had bazaar injuries that facilitated needing an ostomy.

After meeting so many people along the way and hearing tales of life-long battles with bowel diseases, I felt relieved to only have had cancer. Even though I had an extensive seven-hour-long initial surgery, and several more following, I felt I was one of the fortunate ones. I had never taken the time to reflect on that part of my body or its importance since I had never been sick with bowel problems. It was a working organ I took for granted every day of my life until October 2, 1995, when my doctor told me he was almost 100 percent sure I had cancer of the rectum. Before my diagnosis with colorectal cancer, I was clueless about the mechanics of my intestines and never thought of their importance to my everyday comfort.

You'll notice the people that share their stories in this book appear to be talking about their bathroom habits in some detail.

No surprise when you know this book is about ostomy tales and the ostomy pouch collects our waste products. My request was that they share an ostomy related story that was humorous or inspirational. You will see that humor has varying degrees, is subjective, and what is hilarious to one person may not appeal to another person's funny bone. Sometimes just getting back into the swing of an ordinary life can be inspiring. Among the contributors are stories from nurses that work with people living with ostomies. To quote a priest I met many years ago, "Nurses will go straight to heaven." I would have to agree with him. We, as ostomates, love our nurses because they are knowledgeable, kind, and hopeful for us. They won't allow us to feel ashamed or disgusted by having an ostomy; instead, they are our personal cheerleaders encouraging us to accomplish our goals and dreams, or simply do our laundry.

The people living with ostomies in these stories have big lives. They are similar to a lot of people as they juggle families, work, messy houses, and too many desires with never enough time. Having an ostomy has not slowed them down or kept them from trying parachuting or scuba diving. For many, ostomy surgery was a fresh start to a new adventurous life put on hold for too long. Just like others, ostomates love their families, and attend churches, temples, or mosques. They enjoy travel, playing sports, drinking a beer, and just hanging out by the lake—ordinary people, with the exception of having their internal plumbing rearranged. By sharing their funny or intimate moments with their ostomies, they give us a glimpse into a snapshot view of their everyday lives. Even though their stories focus on ostomy-related events, they are much more than their ostomies. They bring hope, humor, and inspiration to the new ostomate or family member reading this book. Their situations may have been critical, but they did not let those experiences make up the entire definition of who they are in life.

Having an ostomy for many of us is what saved our lives. We are grateful to be able to live longer and for many of us—better. If you are contemplating surgery or want to support someone who just had it, know that it takes time to feel comfortable with the whole process. I compare it to driving a car for the first time. Think back to the time when you first got your drivers license. You would get into the car, adjust the seat, the mirrors, *not* turn on the radio, perhaps roll the window down or up, adjust your seat belt, and all this before you even started the ignition. You carefully looked over your shoulders before you gently reversed your car down the driveway. Shifting the gear into place was purposeful and unnatural. The feeling of the brakes beneath your foot was highly responsive. Keenly alert to anything that might happen, you practiced glancing meticulously every five seconds in your rearview and side mirrors while pacing yourself a safe distance from other vehicles. Your hands placed in the "ten and two" positions on the steering wheel, you turned into the proper lanes and always used your signals. Feeling nervous and hypersensitive while you drove, the thought of turning on windshield wipers was intimidating. You may not have even taken a deep breath for a long time. That lasted about a week. Soon, driving became effortless and automatic. The steps you needed to take to get your car down the road were mindful, yet natural.

Changing your pouch at home for the first time is a lot like being a new driver. You review the procedures in your head, use caution, and are sensitive to everyone and everything around you. Carefully, you lay out all the necessary items before beginning. It takes a lot of concentration and energy to remember all the details as instructed by your nurse. That lasts a week or two. Before you know it, you are cruising through a pouch change while talking to your spouse or using the hands-free phone, and it feels natural. You do the steps in order, and precisely, without having to think much about it. You breathe normally.

Routine is something we all strive for once we have been ill. Simple things like sweeping the floor, getting groceries, and taking a bath are often appreciated more than before our illness. We changed by having our plumbing rearranged, but hopefully we changed for the better in more ways than just physical. I seem to stare at the clouds more and try things I always thought would be too difficult. I took up the harp and am training for a long bike ride—not that I'm good at either. I do it for my own enjoyment, but like the tortoise, I just keep lumbering along.

Eleven years ago if someone had told me I would be writing a book about living with an ostomy, my first question would have been, "What's an ostomy?" Since writers often write about what they know, to realize I would have firsthand knowledge about living with an ostomy would have freaked me out. Then, when I found out the subject would be about exploring the funny side of it, my next question would have been, "Is that possible?" I found out it is achievable and a good alternative. It doesn't mean that life is always swell with an ostomy. There are people suffering daily while they struggle to live with an ostomy. Many other people choose to find the humor in the angst of it all, perhaps as a coping mechanism.

Each ostomy is surgically unique and has its own set of challenges and concerns. You can read about the various ostomies at the end of this book with details provided by Hollister Incorporated. For the sake of efficiency, you will notice I refer to people as ostomates along with the latest politically correct term of—people living with an ostomy. I use ostomates as a general term only for efficiency in this book.

There are ostomates that climb mountains, ride in rodeos, play football, have babies, run marathons, and make jokes—everything from A to Z. Many people in this book have one thing in common besides being an ostomate or working with people that have ostomies; they decided to laugh about their predicaments or with their patients. It beats the alternative of spending the rest of your days feeling sorry for yourself. To feel sad is natural and tears can be healing, but at some point we have to get up and get going again. Have you noticed our pity parties are not usually well attended? The people in our lives want us to feel better so we can go dance, go out for dinner, or make love to them again. With soccer games to attend, ironing to do, and grass to mow, there's not much time to feel devastated for ourselves.

Still there are those that would rather die than have the life-saving surgery. Nurses have comforted many people through their fears. Our own imaginations about medical blunders could paralyze us. Life has no guarantees, and things will go wrong.

One time after surgery when my bladder wasn't working the best, I was being called to stage at the local comedy club, "Give a hand for the Twin Cities Funniest Person, Brenda Elsagher." As I walked up to the stage, I involuntarily wet my pants. It was embarrassing, humiliating, surprising, uncomfortable, awkward, and somehow I got through it. Luckily, I had on black pants instead of white ones that night. I don't even remember the jokes I did, but I lived through the experience. I have never heard of anyone dying of humiliation. If that were the case, we would have many bad comics keeling over. I did not shrink up and wither away because of it. I learned from it. You *will* live through a poopy accident in public. I've been there too. Bad things can happen—that's the risk of living, but at least we are alive. When we were kids and fell down, we got right back up, brushed ourselves off, and kept on going. We're just older now. Okay, we may need a hand to get back up, but there is so much fun to be had out there in life. Having an ostomy doesn't need to stop you from doing or being what you want—at least not for long.

I realize as I sit here writing this book, I feel great. No poopy problems, no constipation, no skin issues, and it's a good time for me and my stoma known as "Perry" after the cancer saint, St. Peregrine. It isn't always great. Dealing with unexpected diarrhea or abdominal pain can be a drag.

Enjoy the stories of these many contributors identified by their minute biographies. Where no attribution occurs, the comments are from me. Please, take what you need from these stories, and know that you are not alone in your quest for information or comfort. Having an ostomy doesn't make one a freak. I have a sign from an old Quaker saying in my house, "Live well, laugh often, love much." That sums it up well for me.

Advantages

Advantages to living rectum free:
- Saves on toilet paper
- You never lose thong underwear
- No one can call you an a—hole

Advantages of having a urostomy:
- No waiting in lines at the sports arenas
- Timesaver for an over-the-road truck driver
- You can fish all day long without going back to shore periodically

Advantages of having an ileostomy:
- You have to stay hydrated and drink a lot
- Perfect excuse to not eat the vegetables you always hated, claiming fears of a blockage
- Enjoy eating gas-producing foods without worrying about passing gas

Amateur

One who puts on their pouch for the first time. Their tongue sticks out in concentration, their eyebrows furrow in determination, their hands may shake, and they break out in a cold sweat. Similar to the first time you try to get to second base on a date.

Assemble

Laying out all the parts in the right steps to assemble an ostomy pouch change

Wastebasket
            Little plastic bag
                        Tissue
      Washcloth
            Soap
                        Blow dryer
      Paste
            Powder
                  Scissors
                        Pouch
      Scotch on the rocks

Appreciation

On my first trip out after surgery, I stopped back at the hospital and dropped off huge tins of popcorn in appreciation for the care the nurses had given me. They laughed *with* me about all the weird stuff I was going through. I value the nurse who stood up in St Louis, Missouri, and told me that she informs her patients that she *chose* her profession. It makes patients feel great, knowing that nurse was not stuck with us. Instead, we feel like a million bucks knowing our ET/WOCN* nurses cared enough to get additional education to work with our needs.

*ET, Enterostomal therapist, former and often still used name for the nurses that work with ostomy patient care. WOCN wound, ostomy, continence nurse is the updated name.

Autobahn

We were in a village outside of Cologne getting ready for a farewell dinner when I flipped on the TV and saw large buildings on fire. Tuning into CNN, we learned the enormity of the horror of New York.

Shortly after, all flights were cancelled, and we ended up being stranded in Holland for a week following the terrorist's attacks of 9/11. As a colostomate, I was wearing my last wafer, which normally lasted about six days, so I knew I would have a problem. I tried to convey this to the hotel receptionist. She believed I needed to see a doctor in order to examine me and then prescribe the necessary equipment. I finally drew a sketch of the wafer and then she understood. I went to my room to get a mini pouch and then returned to the front desk so we could measure the flange with a metric ruler. We relayed the size I needed to a local medical supply shop, and we were back in business. Now I needed to get a cab there and back before my bus left.

The cab arrived, a Mercedes, and drove the half hour in the rain on the Autobahn in record-breaking time. After asking other cabbies, my driver found the store, double-parked, and I went inside. The clerk informed me they only took cash so my Visa card would not work. I went outside to talk to the cabbie, "I need to go to get some deutscheMarks at the bank." "How much do you need?" he asked me. "250 deutscheMarks [$125 in U.S. money]," I replied.

He came in with me, pulled out his wallet, and paid the clerk. (Now tell me an American cabbie would loan me that much money.)

The trip back was hair-raising as he sped along the Autobahn on our return, all the while telling me how sorry he was for the American people. He said when he had heard the news he pulled his cab over to the side of the road and cried.

We arrived back at the hotel where the hotel kindly paid the cab fare and gave him the money for supplies, and put the charges on our room. He got a big tip that day.

Hank Thill from St. Louis, Missouri, had surgery in 1997. He's been married to Pat for twenty-five years, and they have a merger of seven grown children. Hank has been a musician since age nine and still plays his baby grand piano every day. When he was sixteen, he had one of the best summers of his life playing with a band on the Mississippi River steamboat. Hank received a degree in agricultural chemistry and worked for Ralston Purina company. He volunteers at church and as an ostomy visitor.

Baptist

I was having my blood drawn at the hospital prior to my operation for colorectal cancer. Conversation flowed with the medical technician drawing my blood. Her grandson's photo with him in his football uniform hung behind her on the wall and we made small talk about him. Soon after, I mentioned that I had colorectal cancer and would be operated on the following week. I told her I was hoping to have a clean surgery and avoid all ostomies if possible. The lab technician's name was Dora and she was a nice woman in her mid-forties. She listened as I talked of my concerns and then said she would like to offer a prayer up for a successful outcome of my cancer after she was done with my draw.

She left for a couple of minutes to deal with the blood sample, came back, and put her hands on my shoulder. I had a lot of people pray for me before but never like this; it was the most inspiring prayer I ever heard in my life. I am not used to praying so freely and aloud as she did. Through her prayer, I really felt the presence of God. I figured she must have been a Baptist from the South; it reminded me of the revival kind of prayers.

I wanted to tell her how impressed I was and to acknowledge her faith. I was awe-inspired. I wanted to say, "You are obviously Baptist."

Instead, I mistakenly said, "You are obviously Black."

I was so shook up. "Dora, I'm sorry, I meant to say, obviously you're Baptist."

After she gave me a strange look like, "who is this moron?" and we both cracked up and laughed and laughed. She then told me she was Pentecostal. I think that prayer could have been the one that saved my life.

Frank Moriarty lives with his wife, Mary, in Plymouth, Minnesota. He had a diagnosis of colorectal cancer, which led to four operations including chemo and radiation. Things didn't go well and Frank ended up with a urostomy and a colostomy. Born and raised in Chicago, Illinois, Frank worked for the JC Penney Company for thirty-six years with most of them being a store manager. He has three children, which prompted the move back to Minnesota to be near his grandchildren. Frank jokes he plays a terrible game of golf as often as he can and enjoys participating in a couple of discussion groups.

Band Aid

For my very last colonoscopy I was in the hospital, and it was St. Patrick's Day. I requested an oversized bandage from my nurse, drew a shamrock on it, and wrote "Happy St. Patrick's Day, Dr. Rowen." I placed it strategically on my bottom where he would have to remove it for my procedure. He was surprised and laughed as he began my colonoscopy. Humor has always helped me get through difficult things in life.

Teresa Pavlakis, of California has a Kock Pouch continent ileostomy, four years. Teresa is a homemaker, wife, and mother and enjoys baking.

Baseball Cap

My sixteen-year-old son, John, has traveled along with me to several United Ostomy Association (UOA) conferences in the past and is used to people living with ostomies. He noticed at the last UOA conference, they had commemorative caps for the board members. He whispered he wanted one and asked me to inquire how he could get one. After I asked Dan, a board member, he told his wife, Marilyn, about it, and she was willing to give hers up to John for the price of a hug.

I wondered if he'd ever wear it. This fall he started wearing it to school. Curious, I asked him, "Doesn't anyone ask you what the United Ostomy Association means?" "All the time," was his reply. "What do you tell them?" I asked. "I just tell them it's an association of people that have an ostomy in common. Then they usually want to know, 'What's an ostomy?' and I tell them it's when people have to wear a bag or pouch because their colon and stuff has been rerouted." "Do they ask you more after that?" I inquired. "Nope," was his quick reply.

Later I thought to myself, he sure has come a long way since he told all the neighborhood kids, "My Mommy poops out of her tummy!"

Beans

December 1, 2004—my twenty-fifth wedding anniversary with my husband, Charlie, was spent in the doctor's office at the University of Minnesota being told I would need a rectal and sigmoid colon resection and permanent colostomy due to rectal cancer. Two weeks later, I had surgery.

My husband comes from a family of nine; they are all married with children and most of them live in our small rural town of Arlington, MN (population 2,000). His mother lives in a large old house that is the gathering ground for our large family. Someone stops by to eat lunch or visit with her each day, and it is a regular stop every Sunday after church. They are a large, boisterous, funny family, filled with love. I have never had a reason to tell a bad mother-in-law story because my husband's mother is the best. Many of the twenty-eight grandchildren live in the area and come around every holiday at the big, old house.

Last November, one of my nieces was selling tea and coffee for a fundraiser at school, and I ordered a bag of coffee beans. We gathered at Grandma Thomes' house on Christmas Eve, and my niece delivered my mocha almond beans to me as I sat in the kitchen. I laid them on the table and carried on eating, drinking, laughing, and talking as we always do, when another sister-in-law entered the room. She always asks how I am doing, how I am feeling, how things are going with me, a general caring concern.

She eyed the coffee bag of beans on the table and said, "Oh, is this your bag?" I quickly picked it up, turned it over, exposing the dark coffee beans and exclaimed, "Yes, and it's full of s—t!" Everyone started to laugh, and Lorie felt a bit embarrassed. She said "Well, I thought maybe you were so comfortable with your bag that you could lay it on the table!" causing everyone to roar with laughter.

Charlie has nicknames for me—the "bag lady" or the "Ostomy queen." When we came home from our support group meeting, he told our kids that I was elected the "Ostomy Queen" and they replied, "Really, how cool, Mom, wow." After about the fourth meeting, I think they realized it was just their dad joking around.

When I went back to work after almost eight weeks of leave after my surgery, I did a little show-and-tell. I have been at the medical center for twenty-five years and knew most people very well. Approaching the different cubicles, I sported a transparent pouch with no stool most of the time, so they could get a good look at my stoma. My coworkers were curious, and I was happy to educate everyone about this new part of my life. People were amazed at my openness. It was an adjustment to go through—I cried when I found out, I cried when I woke up from surgery, and now my crying days are over. I am making the best of it and can joke about it.

One night I was lying on my bed with the TV on. A couple of the kids came in and said, "Mom, what are you doing?" I replied, "Well, I'm taking a s—t. They laughed a little and then said, "You're really lucky, Mom. You can do that wherever and whenever you want, while you're eating, while you're sleeping, even while you're driving—that's cool." I replied, "Yup, everyone should have a bag.

Brenda and Charlie Thomes of Minnesota have five children from ages thirteen to twenty years old. Brenda works in the Sibley Medical Center doing transcriptions. In her spare time, she likes to lie on the beach in Cancun sipping pina coladas and reading good books. In real life, though, she spends time cleaning, cooking, doing laundry, along with attending kids' activities and spending time with family and friends—smarting off and enjoying every minute of it.

Benny Goodman

Stomas seem male because they don't mind making rude noises in public; they're almost proud of their indiscriminate farts. Ladies never do that. My stoma has those characteristics, so I named it Benny Goodman because it toots a lot.

Sue Mueller lives in New Mexico, has a colostomy due to cancer. A nurse, wife, and mother, she is very involved with her local ostomy support group and is pursuing a goal of becoming a WOCN.

Big Butt

I had to get over very quickly my self-consciousness about my big butt. With such a traumatic diagnosis of colorectal cancer at age thirty-nine, you would have thought I would have been overwhelmed with survival. Instead, with each new doctor, I would wonder, is this the biggest butt they have ever seen? Do they even notice butts anymore? How many butts has this person seen in their lifetime? What must it be like to spend the day looking into people's butts all day long?

Many lives have been saved by a simple colonoscopy procedure and when cancer happens and it's in the rectum, there's no more time for pride, modesty, and all the dialogue that goes on inside of us. As each exam continued, I would have to say to myself, this is just another butt, no big deal. When I found out my butt cheeks would be sewn together at surgery, I knew one thing for sure—the problem with my nightgown being swallowed between my cheeks was over. There *is* always something positive if you look hard enough.

Bling-Bling

My gregarious friend Shirley Reitmeier, the accessorizing queen, is all about the glitz and glamour. We were talking about it being my ten-year anniversary of being an ostomate. In celebration, Shirley suggested we get some bling-bling for my ostomy or at least glitter up my bag. She says, "If you can't lose it, decorate around it. It's all about accessorizing. Who needs a Louis Vuitton bag when you have a Brenda bag already?"

Camping

Back in the days when patients were in the hospital for longer stays, ten days to two weeks was normal for a colectomy/colostomy. You really got a chance to get to know your patients and see their progression of dealing with their medical issues. A forty-four-year-old patient and mother of four had a diagnosis of cancer and her prognosis was not good. Initially, like most, she really had trouble with the whole cancer deal, but unlike many, she was very open about her feelings.

We were in the hospital room bathroom during the irrigation procedure one morning when she asked, "Will I be able to continue camping with my family?" I assured her with some planning and adaptation, she should be able to join her family and resume their good times together. I'll never forget her light-hearted response when she looked up and said, "In other words, have bag will travel!" I just about lost it. It marked the beginning of a new outlook for her. She was over the hump with self-care after that. The next day I slipped into her room to find her sleeping; at least I thought she was asleep. Before I could turn to leave, she opened her eyes, smiled mischievously, and reported, "I have already been up, completed my irrigation and bag change, and am done for the day." It never ceases to amaze me how the human spirit rises to meet the challenges of life.

San Short, of Thomaston, Georgia, is a fourteen-year colon cancer survivor, wife, and mother of two college kids and loves to travel. San is an Auburn University fanatic and volunteers for the Relay for Life for the American Cancer Society. She has been an ostomy nurse for over twenty-five years.

Carpet

Linda and I were dating, and she was flying into Philadelphia for a meeting. I went to meet her at the airport. After I parked in the parking lot, I headed toward her arrival gate, and as I walked there, I suddenly felt a hot rush down my leg. I started shaking my foot and found that my clip had come undone and was now lying in the corner of the stairwell. Fortunately, no one was around, so I made a temporary fix-up job long enough to get back to my car. I looked around for an extra pair of pants, but I could only find a piece of carpet that was eighteen inches wide and six feet long. I took it out and held it over my arm like a waiter would hold a towel, and I proceeded down past the security to meet Linda.

The security guard saw me holding the carpet. "Sir, can I see your other arm?" I shifted my arms keeping the carpet still in place. He questioned, "Can I ask what this is all about?" Without hesitation, I said, "One of my salesmen is coming in and has performed badly, and I am calling him on the carpet." I proceeded with a smile on my face through security and went to meet Linda at the gate. She looked at the carpet, took a sniff of the air, and said, "What is going on?" "Come with me and let's go home," I said, and we quickly made our exit.

Ken Aukett has had an ileostomy since 1972, due to ulcerative colitis. Ken is an active volunteer in both national and international ostomy support efforts and led the steering committee for the United Ostomy Associations of America, formed in 2005. He and Linda (also living with an ostomy) married in 1988 and live in New Jersey. They enjoy managing a small business, traveling, camping, and helping others.

Caulking

After my initial three-week intensive training at Hollister Incorporated, studying many cases of stomas, ostomies, and treatment, I dreamt I needed to have a stoma. In my dream, I told the doctor how to make it, where to put it, and how far it should protrude. It surprised me when I awoke and found I did not have one.

As a sales specialist, I often attend ostomy support meetings. One ostomy patient confided that he was having problems with a particular pouch. It would only last three days. I had an extra pouch with me. "Show me how you prepare your skin and then how you apply the pouch to it." He told me he cleaned and dried his skin gently. He then took the pre-sized convex pouch, took off the backing on the tape, and placed it on his abdomen. "Did you remember to release the plastic layer over the barrier?" I questioned, thinking he did not want to ruin my sample. He said, "I'm suppose to take that off too?" He was pleased to know he would now get more wear time.

I learn a lot from the patients, too. Soon after I started, a patient told me the ostomy paste should be renamed "caulking." He told me that when it comes to paste, more was not better, too much would make it fall off. Use it more like filling caulk in a crack. Those have been words of wisdom for me.

A Minnesota native, LaDonna Cleveland has been with Hollister Incorporated since 1983 and has seen great technical improvements every year in the field of ostomy products. In her spare time, she enjoys gardening and refinishing antique furniture.

Children

My children were three and five when I was diagnosed with cancer. They inspired me to get up and get moving when I didn't feel like it. Now they are teens, and *I* have to inspire *them* to get up and get moving when *they* don't feel like it.

Chitchat

Seniors in my neighborhood in Florida often sidle up to me and say in hushed tones, "Are you the lady that knows all about colons?" I smile, stifle a giggle, and ask them how I can help. Telling people I have a colostomy is part of the talks I give and the writing I do about colorectal cancer prevention with an emphasis on *life* since I have been a cancer survivor since 1988.

Recently my husband and I were traveling in Australia. While waiting for our room keys in a hotel lobby in Sydney, a woman approached and pointed to my large red canvas bag and bellowed out, "Are you an ET?" "No," I replied in a somewhat startled voice, "But I do have an ostomy." "I do, too," she chattered. My big red bag had come from a WOCN conference that I attended and was just the right size to carry all our medications and my ostomy supplies. I had forgotten about the large lettering on the side that identified the Wound Ostomy Continence Nurses Society.

I asked her when she had surgery. "Just six months ago," she replied. When I revealed that my colostomy surgery had been seventeen years ago and that I was traveling from America, she was overwhelmed. "I can grow old with this, " she marveled. "And travel and experience life," I added. She gave me a hug and walked out the hotel door with a grin spreading across her sweet face. I smiled, too, over this chance encounter, a provocative chitchat about ostomies in a public place. I never dreamed that I might be making a difference in someone's life a million miles from home.

The Traveler

Ten weeks after surgery,
Healing body, adventurous spirit
On its way to New Zealand,
Stops to refresh on a fragrant Tahiti beach.
Pouch hidden beneath vibrant suit,
Dips into tropical water.
Barriers hold fast in the hot humid paradise.

Onward to winter on the other side of the world.
Flying away, a busman's holiday
Visiting schools down under.
Filling the void of disease with images
Pulsating with life.
Deer farms, trout pools,
A glow worm grotto twinkling in the dark
Of a crisp winter day.
Maori songs and Hangi feast illuminate the night.

Dairy farms without flies, litter-free byways.
School tots in stocking feet
With shoes outside the door.
Sheep dogs atop the flock
Dash to the tune of the whistler.
A topsy turvy view of life so far away from home.

I'm a traveler, a survivor,
Finding wonder in the ordinary.

Ann M. Favreau

Normalcy

Nobody knows she isn't whole,
With pouch beneath her dress.
She stands before an audience
That she will soon address.
Nobody knows he isn't whole.
This young man in his teens,
Playing ball and having fun
In bathing suit and jeans.
Pouches give them confidence,
Light barriers from strife.
Plastic holds their secret,
As they go on living life.

Ann M. Favreau

Ann M. Favreau had a colostomy as a result of colorectal cancer in 1988. She knows that surviving is an active journey. Her travels have taken her around the world, to the White House, and into the hearts of ostomates and cancer survivors through her poetry, writing, and personal visits. Ann held leadership positions in the United Ostomy Association rising to president in 2000 and was honored in 2003 with the Sam Dubin Award, the highest volunteer award given by UOA. In 2005, she received the President's Award. Ann is a mother and grandmother and lives with her husband in Florida.

Decorated

In 1980, I was a brand new ET, and I was helping a patient with colostomy irrigation. I was scared, meticulous, and barely knew what to do, but we were getting through it all very well. In those days, I used to wear three-inch spiked heels and short skirts. At that time in the medical field, we started teaching people to irrigate from their beds on day five in the hospital. Now we never do that. After my patient's successful colostomy irrigation procedure, I took the bedpan to empty it, and I slipped. The bedpan went up in the air and all that success was all over my face, my hair, and my lab coat; I was fully decorated. When the patient looked at me and I looked at him; we were both so shocked, we burst out laughing. I cleaned up as best I could, put on some scrubs, and continued with work.

The whole idea of a colostomy is nothing to me. The by-product does not bother me—it's nothing; it's the person I care about. Imagine poop all over my skirt and hair, but we were able to laugh heartily. There is nothing bad about poop or pee except when we can't do it; that's the only time it's bad.

Pat Keegan, ET/ WOCN since 1979, lives in Minnesota and is a proud mom of two kids with her first grandchild on the way. Pat has been in private practice since 1989, claiming she has the best job in the world. In her spare time, she travels through the United States and watches her friend Jerry play softball.

Dogs

Sistah Stoma is the name of my stoma because, although I'm white on the outside and have no proper sense of funk and rhythm, I figure that maybe my intestine does—so she's the stylin' Sistah Stoma.

A lot of my friends have been curious to poke the Sistah to see her squirm in response. It's great for show-and-tell for people, particularly about things they've never seen before that might be considered gross.

Dogs are inquisitive too. Dogs naturally will gravitate to the usual places and seem to linger longer with me than with other people. It's hard to explain to the random person on the street why their dog is so interested in me and even harder to explain to the dog.

Christine Armer of Oregon met her ileostomy in 2005 at thirty-five years old due to Crohn's Disease. After spending thirty years in school (preschool through a PhD in Entomology), she dropped out of the career track and became a homemaker who gets to sleep in every day, figure out life and the direction she's headed. Christine says, "A life-changing disease made things harder in some ways, and easier in others." She's made time to have a dog, knit, quilt, and works on stained glass projects and woodworking.

Double Bagger

I was born with cloacal-exstrophy, (when the bladder and colon are on the outside of the body at birth), and that is the reason I have two ostomies. I'll admit it; I'm a "double bagger." At birth I also had a condition similar to hip displasia and had an opening at the base of the spine. Surgery was required to close the base of my spine, and then they performed surgery for an ileostomy and a urinary diversion as well. They actually left an opening in my abdomen. There wasn't a stoma, but an opening where my parents had to vigilantly watch over my skin and put zinc oxide ointment under a baggie and secure it with tape; I wasn't expected to live.

I was in the hospital for three months after I was born. At six months old, I had ileostomy surgery, and at two years old, had a ureter ostomy made from the urinary diversion and have had two ostomies since.

There have been many surgeries, but I have scuba-dived, water-skied, rafted, snowmobiled, jet-skied, and traveled. Overall, I'm very healthy even though I had over twenty surgeries before I was twenty years old.

One of my passions has been to volunteer as a counselor at youth camp. I love being with kids that have the same challenges I faced as a child with an ostomy. There was one camper, a shy young girl, whose parents had told her that she would probably never be able to date because of her ostomy. When she found out that I had two ostomies and that I was married, she quietly asked me, "Does he know?" I wanted to laugh, but I knew she was serious. I told her, "Yes he does, and it doesn't matter." I could see the relief instantly come over her face, and that made me so happy to be able to help her.

Because of attending meetings involving ostomates around the world, I have friends from all over the globe. I once met a woman from Belgium who also had two ostomies. I think the wine we shared over dinner made us less inhibited because in no time at all we were in the bathroom comparing scars and ostomy surgeries. It was the first time I ever saw a mirror image of myself.

Fifteen years ago my mom had an ostomy due to cancer. Radiation treatment had caused damage to her intestines. After trying medications for two years and symptoms of colitis, she convinced her doctors to give her an ostomy. It's not your typical mother-daughter experience, but it is a special bond.

JoAnne Sisco lives in Minnesota with her husband, Don, and their daughter, Abby. She works for the American Heart Association and in her spare time, she enjoys decorating, shopping, scrapbooking, and reading.

Duct tape

There are a million uses for duct tape. One time when I was on a houseboat with ten women cruising down the mighty Mississippi River, we turned a little too late and accidentally hit a government dredge. They don't move since they are solid iron. The boat was damaged but still drivable. The men from the dredge came on board and looked at the hole. We found some duct tape, patched it up, and went on our merry way; however, we lost our damage deposit that year.

Since that time I have found many other uses for duct tape as well. I was at a St. Patrick's Day party and was eating dinner when I detected a foul smell. I covertly reached down to touch my pouch under my pants and realized I had a leak. I quickly exited the table, got my purse, and was thankful I always carried extra supplies. It had never happened to me before and, as I laid out the pieces I would need to do a pouch change, I saw that I had forgotten the clip for the end of the pouch. I discreetly called out to my friend Corinne, " Can you ask Don (the host and an electrician) if he has any duct tape?" I figured that if it could keep a boat afloat for three days, duct tape should be able to hold my pouch together until I got home.

Pretty soon, the guests at the table got wind of my request for duct tape, and I could hear them all making jokes about what is she doing in the bathroom with duct tape? Many of them did not know me well. I heard my friend Corinne who had been with me through tests and turmoil with my ostomy surgery say, "She had cancer and has a colostomy, and she forgot the clip to close the end of the pouch so she wants something strong to keep it shut." Their mouths closed so fast, and they were all embarrassed that they had been joking. I could hear all this through the bathroom door. Naturally, when I came out of the bathroom they were giving me those sympathetic glances or trying to eyeball where my ostomy was on my body. It was awkward to say the least. I sat down to continue eating without them being aware that I knew they were told I had a colostomy. To end the uncomfortable moment, I proposed a toast. "To duct tape," I said. Then everyone repeated it while we laughed and carried on with our night.

Dutiful Nurse

During my sister's recovery from surgery resulting in a temporary colostomy, we tackled her round-the-clock care with a team made up of my mother, Nancy's fiancée James, and me. Unsure of my nursing abilities, I knew I could offer two things: comic relief with my four-year-old daughter, Rachel, and a more flexible schedule as a stay-at-home mom.

Atlantans are familiar with an eatery downtown known for chili dogs and greasy onion rings. For years, there have been jokes about how going to this establishment for an "oil and lube job" could cause a major "colon blow." After Nancy's surgery, she assured us that she had eaten at a local sandwich shop, not the place we feared had done her damage.

Even though Nancy's stoma was temporary, she named it Ted, which quickly developed his own personality and was a source of blame for more than he deserved. Nancy also came home with a catheter that needed emptying. Challenged to be the dutiful nurse and loving sister, I was ready. Like any good nurse, I donned latex gloves—bodily fluids were involved and love only goes so far. Nancy clamped it off, and I attempted to pull the tube out. To our great dismay, the clamp failed and urine went everywhere—on the floor, on Nancy's leg, on me, and on her favorite recuperation chair.

As Nancy's condition improved, so did her disposition. Rachel and Nancy share not only a love for each other, but also the *Wizard of Oz*, *A Baby Story* on TLC, and catchy songs. I believe two factors led to Nancy's speedy recovery—the many prayers on her behalf and heavy doses of humor.

Reflecting back on Nancy's current attachments, I took sisterly pleasure in teasing her about multi-tasking. She could talk on the phone, prepare a sandwich, and use the restroom simultaneously without pausing to observe additional personal hygiene.

The incision made during surgery resulted in the loss of Nancy's belly button. Thinking that was weird, Rachel got excited when the latest *Veggie Tales* release had a silly song with the line, "Baby, I need to tell you something. I don't got a belly button." We laughed when we heard it and declared it Nancy's theme song. A time forever etched in our minds, we are appreciative of being able to help nurse Nancy back to good health. Younger sisters look up to their older sisters as role models, and Nancy has been a great example for us.

Susan Lukavsky was a caregiver to her sister recuperating from a temporary colostomy in 2003. She spends most of her time taking care of her husband and kids and is involved at church where her husband is a deacon.

Envy

I had a surgery that failed after four weeks, and at the time of the second surgery when they removed my entire colon, it had deteriorated to the extent of having only one inch of healthy tissue remaining. The ulcerative colitis had damaged it so dramatically, it was a wonder I didn't develop cancer. The next procedure was a traditional ileostomy.

A year later, the stoma prolapsed (stuck out) to the point that a person could have penis envy. My grandson followed me to the bathroom one time. When I pulled down my pants, my four-year-old grandchild asked, "Grandma, you have a penis?"

"No, grandmothers don't have those," I answered.

He continued, "My daddy does, and his is very big."

My stoma's name is Stella; she even speaks Stellanese. She has her own song to the tune of "Sally was a Good Ole Girl." We've been together ten years now. My granddaughter thinks all grandmothers have Stellas. She asked me, "When I am a grandma, do I get a Stella too?" She used to lift up people's shirts looking for them.

I love it when you're in the hospital or the doctor's office and they ask you, "Have you had a bowel movement lately?" I usually respond with, "Oh, as we speak."

My father never told me that he loved me. I found out he loved me when I had my second ileostomy and had an accident where the bag came off and the s—t hit the fan, literally. I saw my father on his hands and knees cleaning it up without ever fussing at me. He never said it, but he showed it.

Buni Weller and her husband, Allen, live in Hendersonville, Tennessee. Buni enjoys cross-stitching—it goes back to her hairdresser days when she could see the before and after. She loves to play with her grandchildren and bargain hunt at thrift stores. Buni likes to go to church at the United Methodist Church where Allen is the minister.

Experience

I had been putting on my pouches for over thirty years. Recently my wife had some medical problems and ended up with a temporary ostomy. After Barbara came home from the hospital, I helped her with her appliance change. Several hours later, we were shocked when it leaked. With all my experience, I had forgotten to take the paper off the adhesive back of the pouch.

George and Barbara Salamy from New Jersey have helped many people over the years through their local and national ostomy associations.

Fair

As a new ostomate, I attended my local ostomy support group and shortly afterward started receiving newsletters and other information. I got a flyer on an upcoming Appliance Fair. I assumed it had to do with refrigerators, stoves, and dishwashers. I live in an apartment and those items are included in the rent, so I thought an appliance fair was of no use to me.

Thinking it was odd that an ostomy group would send a flyer for that, I glanced at the flyer again, and then realized I had misunderstood and the Appliance Fair was for people to learn about various ostomy products. When I went to the fair, I shared my story with WOCN, Pat Keegan. She put her arm around me and said, "Oh, honey—you really are a rookie, aren't you?"

Debbie Hull, of Minnesota, was a typical healthy twenty-year-old when she suddenly became ill with Crohn's Disease in December, 1977. In 1984, she had ileostomy surgery and has been well ever since. Debbie says, "All the bad memories have faded, I can do anything I want: travel, work, exercise, eat what I want—life is good. I am grateful there was a solution for my situation."

Finger Wave

I received this song so many times over the Internet, I decided to track down the songwriters in Canada to ask if I might share the lyrics with the readers. I urge you to go to their website to listen to it.

Working Where the Sun Don't Shine

We praise the colorectal surgeon,
Misunderstood and much maligned,
Slaving away in the heart of darkness,
Working where the sun don't shine

Respect the colorectal surgeon,
It's a calling few would crave,
Lift up your hands and join us,
Let's all do the finger wave.

When it comes to spreading joy,
There are many techniques,
Some spread joy to the world,
Others just spread cheeks.

Some may think the cardiologist
Is their best friend,
But the colorectal surgeon knows
He'll get you in the end.

Why be a colorectal surgeon?
It's one of those mysterious things.
Is it because in that profession
There are always openings?

When I first met a colorectal surgeon,
He did not quite understand.
I said "Hey, it's nice to meet you,
But do you mind if we don't shake hands?"

He sailed right through medical school,
Because he was a whiz.

But he never thought of psychology
When he read *Passages*.

A doctor he wanted to be,
For golf he loved to play.
But this is not quite what he meant
By eighteen holes a day.

Respect the colorectal surgeon,
Here and now we'll raise a glass,
For the rectal surgeon, like the rectum,
Can tell a liquid from a gas.

We praise the colorectal surgeon,
Misunderstood and much maligned.
Slaving away in the heart of darkness,
Working where the sun don't shine.

Words and music by George Bowser and Rick Blue
From the CD Humour for Boomers, *by Bowser and Blue*

George Bowser and Rick Blue have been writing and performing music and comedy together since 1978. Colorectal surgeons around the world are familiar with them through the song "Working Where the Sun Don't Shine," which was first heard on "Madly Off In All Directions" in 1997. To hear the artists sing this song, go to their website at www.bowserandblue.com.

Flat Rides

An avid sailor from Massachusetts, Alvin McMahon, didn't let his ileostomy keep him off the water. Before his ostomy surgery, Alvin was part of a crew that sailed on a racing boat called "Aggressive." His job on the team was to be the grinder, a position which meant when the boat changed direction, he would grind the winches to pull the jib sail over to the windward side. Immediately after grinding, which was done from the cockpit, Alvin would climb out quickly and go to the upper rail. Weight was needed on the highest rail so the boat didn't tip over. In a race, it typically was heeled over at forty degrees, which means there is not a flat surface in the boat. This challenging climb must be done at the same angle at lightning speed.

After a quick recovery from ileostomy surgery, Alvin's doctor said he could resume anything he was doing before he had the operation. He thought about his job as a sailor and the aggressive manner in which they sailed. Concerned about a potential disaster during racing if he slipped on the run up to the rail and ripped open the pouch or accidentally nicked his stoma, he revised his plans. Not one to quit being a sailor, he charted out a new direction.

Even though Alvin loved racing, he decided to spend his sailing days on calm water using "iron sails"—he runs a motor and no sails. Just like the wind, Alvin didn't waste any time changing directions. He baby-sits big yachts, runs the engines, and takes the boats out for the owners who occasionally appear. Ironically, he gave up something he enjoyed but actually does more boating now. The advantage of "flat rides" is that he gets to sit up straight for a change and take in the view in a more relaxed pace. Alvin still enjoys getting together with his sailing crew to talk about the races but has no regrets. When he's not at the marina, you'll find him volunteering for his local police department. Having ostomy surgery might have changed his course, but it looks like smooth sailing now.

Alvin McMahon, has been an ileostomate for two years. After thirty-two years in the airline business, he still likes to travel and recently became a grandfather. In his spare time, he helps at the local ostomy group and enjoys being on the pit crew for classic car racing.

Flying Clamp

One beautiful fall day, my husband and I were at our cabin in the northern woods of Wisconsin. It was mid-morning, and we expected company later that day. Bustling around, I wanted everything ready when they arrived, postponing a growing need as my pouch filled.

Then the telephone rang. I sat down to listen to my brother as he conveyed important family information. Meanwhile, my ignored need kept growing and suddenly, with a whoosh, I deflated. I figured the wafer lost its grip, pushed off by pressurized gas. I put my hand over the location of the wafer, kept my composure, and finished the conversation.

As I headed for the bathroom, I stopped in shock. On the floor near my chair lie a pristine white ostomy clamp. With a quick fingertip exploration through my blue jeans, I realized it wasn't a wafer problem at all. My composure vanished as I hobbled to the privacy of my bathroom.

Happily, when the guests arrived, I was cleaned up with a new resolve to explode no more and a vow to myself to make bathroom visits more frequently to avoid the big build-up.

A few weeks after the episode of the flying clamp, hubby and I were driving the two-hour drive home from the cabin. At a Holiday Station stop, I used the restroom to empty my gas, mindful of my recent lesson learned. On we went. He drove, I crocheted, car filled, pouch emptied.

Soon we were home in our garage and, as I began to unkink my arthritic knees, I stared in disbelief. Another ostomy clamp lie on the garage floor—thirty years without incident had changed. Logic dictated I didn't fasten the clamp properly, now I needed to restore confidence with a reinforcement that came as a metal binder clip, sold in office supply stores. I put it on top of the white plastic clamp—no more single-clamp system for me. I forge ahead, empty, clamp, hope, smile, and laugh at new surprises.

Judith Lippold had a sigmoid colostomy in 1975 due to rectal cancer. Retired from occupational therapy and her husband from being a professor of broadcast journalism, they enjoy their two daughters, sons-in-law, and four grandchildren. Judith is a facilitator of Renewing Life, a program for people with life-threatening or chronic illness and enjoys reading, editing the ostomy newsletter, artwork, and memoir writing.

Free Willie

My stoma's name is Willie. Rather than having a cute little stoma button, lucky me, my surgeon decided to make mine a little longer. I ended up with one that looks like a miniature penis about the length of my pinky. When Willie gets active, he gets erect, looking even more like a little boy's penis, and that is why I call him little Willie. It's rather appropriate when I change my pouch, I then " free Willie."

A few years ago, the national ostomy conference was in Reno. One evening some of the girls were trying to explain to a guy in the hotel bar what our conference was about. He was really nice; he seemed really interested, but he just was not getting it! I was wearing a front-buttoned denim skirt; I discreetly turned so that only he could see and much to the horror of the ostomates who surrounded us, I whipped my skirt open to show him my clear pouch. Thank God, I had just emptied and cleaned it so that he could be introduced to little Willie. You could actually see the light bulb go on. He wasn't grossed out or anything. In fact, he was fascinated. My show-and-tell still gets an honorable mention each year at the conference.

Gayle Stowe was diagnosed with Ankylosing Spondylitis (or AS) in 1986, a chronic disease that causes inflammation in the joints, often causing fusing and curving of the spine. A severe bout of Ulcerative Colitis in 1989 resulted in Gayle receiving an ileostomy. While she was in the hospital, she joined the Bermuda chapter of the UOA where she served as membership secretary and later as treasurer. She represented North America in helping to organize the first 20/40 (age) conference held in Copenhagen in 1999. She is currently a member of the new UOAA's (United Ostomy Association of America) 30+ Committee.

Gayle celebrated the seventeenth anniversary of her twenty-ninth birthday last October. She lives in Bermuda, a group of islands off the coast of North Carolina, and works for a local insurance company. Gayle loves life and finds joy in reading, dancing, and travel.

Gifts

My son had recently moved to Washington D.C., so we communicated mostly by phone for several months following my surgery. The Christmas holidays approached and we discussed gifts. Jokingly, I told him I wanted a new colon. Christmas morning arrived, and he presented me with a rolled up paper, like a tube. When I unrolled it, there were two dots, one over the other like : I looked at it and said, "Thank you, but what is it?" He said, "I have given you a new 'colon' like you requested." It was the best laugh I had in months.

Sue Brown, of Worcester, Massachusetts, has been an ileostomate since September 1999. She has one child and is a special education teacher that works with students who are too ill to attend school daily.

God

Why me?
    Why *not* me?

Good News and Bad News

My older sister Carolyn was having a heart cath, and my sisters Kathy and Marsha and I decided to make the trip to Columbia to be with her. We arrived after a two-hour trip from Charlotte before she got to the hospital, and the nurses generously offered to let us stay in her assigned room.

As we sat there waiting, a nurse walked in, looked straight at me and said, "I need to get you in a gown." I informed her I was not the victim—I mean patient. A few minutes later, another nurse came in and tried to take blood out of me. When Carolyn finally arrived, we informed her that we had good news and bad news for her. The good news was they thought I was her, and my heart was in excellent shape. The bad news was if that was true, someone had stolen her rectum! The nurses got a good laugh too.

Diana Boyles of North Carolina has been married to the love of her life for thirty-seven years. They have two children, a granddaughter, and another on the way. In 1995, after several operations and hospitalizations, she had a colostomy. Six months later, she exchanged it for an ileostomy She says, "Most people only have one birthday, I have two. My life began again, with some limitations, but for the most part pain free and much healthier!" She got through her hard times with family, church, and the love of her man, Charles.

GYGIG

I had been training in June 2005, for the Get Your Guts in Gear bike ride held in New York. The week before the bike ride, my wife and I were up at New York's Columbia Presbyterian hospital in upper Manhattan at a United Ostomy meeting. After we parked the car, we walked up a steep hill, and I saw a biker on top of it. "Can you believe that?" I said. "I don't think I could ride up this hill. I would have to walk my bike up." The next week for the GYGIG ride, I surprised myself when we rode up to the same point of that hill, and I was able to ride all the way up. I participated in the 210-mile GYGIG (Get Your Guts in Gear) bike ride for the purpose of increasing awareness of IBD (Inflammatory Bowel Disease), which includes Crohn's Disease and ulcerative colitis and the sometimes resulting ostomy surgery. I suffered from ulcerative colitis for five years. Medications were not successful, so I elected to have a standard ileostomy that changed my life.

After meeting Judith Pacitti, the founder of GYGIG, ride director, and Crohn's sufferer herself, and some serious soul searching, I thought—why not? Though I was a bit older than most riders were, I thought it might illustrate to others that people living with an ostomy can do this ride like anyone else. Even though there were sixty-two riders, I was the only ostomate riding. Most of the other riders had some form of IBD or were riding for a friend or family member who suffered from Crohn's or colitis.

I participated in this ride for ostomates out there reluctant to try something new and for those who don't want others to know they have an ostomy. The way we will be comfortable talking about these diseases and ostomy surgery is to help the general public understand that having ostomy surgery is a positive thing, giving us a new lease on life so we can continue living life to the fullest.

Despite the pouring rain at the start of the ride, 92-degree heat, and being a beginner cyclist, I was physically prepared and mentally ready to participate. I used a two-piece appliance, and I was able to empty the pouch at the regular stops. I did not have to empty more than normal; in fact, I only had to empty three times during the riding part of the day. I changed the appliance once the first evening and was good to go the rest of the ride.

A benefit to the ride was getting to know the other riders. As the only ostomate riding (others were on the support crew), I had the opportunity to discuss what it was like to ride with an appliance. I think most of the riders thought it was quite a feat even though it really wasn't anything exceptional—another reason to educate the public. Maybe I was able to help others to make an educated decision on surgery if necessary. The main reason I rode was to prove that those of us with ostomies are not different and, in fact, have a greater quality of life than those suffering with serious diseases.

This was my New York marathon, and I am pleased that I finished it. Over one hundred friends and relatives contributed to my ride and had a hand in increasing the awareness of Inflammatory Bowel Disease and ostomy surgery. Now all you ostomates, I urge you to get out there and ride—you can do it!

George Salamy of New Jersey, had ileostomy surgery in 1976. He says, "It was a new lease on life, which has allowed me to live a very fruitful and exciting life." At the time of surgery, George had recently married Barbara, an RN who understood and was supportive. They have three daughters. George worked for nearly thirty years for AT&T, traveling the world—even to third world countries with limited sanitation back in the 1980s. He says his ileostomy is not limiting because he often plays golf, swims, and we know he can ride a bike.

Handicapped Bathroom

An usher at the theater downtown would guard the handi-capped bathroom and only let "handicapped" people in to use it before or during the plays. When I walked toward the door, she said, "This bathroom is for handicapped people only." Am I handicapped I thought? No, but I knew the bathrooms upstairs had no sinks in the stalls, and I had not brought things with me that I would need. Instead, I said, "Some handicaps cannot be seen. Although I am not handicapped like some people, I would prefer to use a toilet with a sink in the same room." She seemed perplexed, but I would have done a show-and-tell and embarrassed her if I needed to get my point across. Luckily, she stepped aside.

Help

Awareness about ostomies has changed a lot in twenty years. I recall a woman needing help because she didn't have any ostomy supplies. It was a dire situation so I called a local phar-macy. "Do you have any ostomy supplies?" I asked. The phar-macist responded, "No, but if you tell me what they are, we can get them for you on our next order." He was trying to be help-ful, but clueless until I explained what we needed. He realized the bandages he was offering were not going to work. Instead, we used my stuff and made it work until Monday when she could get an appointment to see the ET.

LaVerna Reid has had an ileostomy since 1972 due to ulcerative colitis. She has been married forty-two years, is a grandmother to five, and is a recipient of the Sam Dubin Award. It is the highest award given out by the United Ostomy Association. She is active in her community and church choir and an important resource of information for ostomates. She owns a printing company in Edmond, Oklahoma.

High Fives

My surgery for colon cancer and ostomy was on December 23. I felt sorry for anyone having to work over the Christmas holiday, so I purchased a bunch of little treats, wrapped them, and started giving them out to anyone that took care of me. Before I knew it, total strangers were standing in my room. Some didn't  even pretend to fiddle with my IV or other equipment. I would ask them, "Did you want a gift?" They would nod, and I'd say, "Help yourself." It was fun for me. Apparently the word had gotten out that it was pretty good candy. My life-long saying is, "We are all a bunch of funny people." They sure proved it that day.

After surgery, the doctor came in to give me the good news that the lymph nodes were not involved. My husband was in the corner crying because he was so happy. I don't think the doctor knew about high fives; he seemed perplexed and ended up shaking my hand at head level.

Audrey Paul, colon cancer survivor and colostomate since 2002, is married with two wonderful sons and adorable granddaughters. A former teacher, and past owner of an ambulance company, she loves reading, quilting, Sudoku, and going to their cabin in northern Minnesota.

Humor

Most of the time, I coped with my ostomy and colon cancer with humor. It seemed to relax me as well as those around me. It gave them permission to tease me when they saw I could laugh about it. Conversations were less strained because we didn't pretend; we just dealt with it head on using a well-placed laugh.

Hunting

In Michigan, deer hunting season begins November 15 each year. Even though it was only three weeks post-op of my third and, hopefully, last ileostomy, I planned to go on my first hunt about 150 miles from my home. I asked my surgeon if it would be okay to go, and he gave me permission with two caveats: have someone else drag out the deer and bring back two steaks for him.

We had set up blinds in September so the animals would acclimate to this new thing in their area. Mine was in a low, wooded spot adjacent to a recently cut cornfield, approximately three quarters of a mile from where we could park the "Jimmy."

On November 14, a great Michigan snowstorm blew in and left eight inches of white fluffy snow—a deer hunter's dream setting! Early the next day, my wife made a great breakfast, and I started dressing for the adventure and very cold opening day.

First, came the two-piece red silk underwear, followed by two-piece thermal weave underwear, followed by a turtleneck sweater, and blue jeans. Then came the hunter orange quilted bib overalls and orange hunting jacket, followed by insulated socks, waterproof footwear, hat, and gloves.

My wife made a thermos of coffee for me while I prepared my hand warmers—metal things filled with cotton that you soaked with lighter fluid, lit, and carried in a red flannel pouch. Finally ready, I drove to our targeted area before dawn, earlier than the deer awoke, and slogged through the foot of snow.

Sitting on the stool in the blind, I enjoyed my morning coffee as I watched the skies lighten while keeping my hands toasty with the hand warmers in my jacket pockets.

This was the life. An hour passed and then—bang! I shot my first buck. I waited to make sure he was down for the count and slowly ventured from the blind. Astonished, as I moved, I felt the dreaded warm trickle from the belt line up and down. Then I realized, the hand warmer in my right pocket was directly over my ostomy flange and had completely melted the adhesive.

It didn't take long to decide what to do. I trudged through the snow, got to my car, and headed back the few miles to the shack. After I got into the bathtub, I started peeling off all those layers of clothes. I laughed as I stood in the shower washing off my clothes and me. My wife thought I was crazy and started laughing too. After cleaning up, I got a friend with me to drag the deer out of the cornfield. I was able to field dress it on the spot, but I needed help to move it. Then we took it to the processing shop to have it butchered. When I arrived back home, I made the promised delivery to Doc Ferguson at his office. That was a memorable first day of hunting.

Dan C. Tyrrell of Michigan had his third ostomy surgery October of 1989, due to a ruptured bowel caused by diverticulitis. He has been married to Marilyn forty-nine years. They have three married children with five grandchildren. Dan loves fishing even more than hunting. He retired from General Motors at age fifty-three, and worked for another twelve years building custom homes. An active member of UOA, Dan was on the board of directors and was a Sam Dubin award winner.

Icebreaker

When I was recovering from my first ostomy surgery in 1995, I started thinking about how I would tell the women from my Bible study group about my surgery. I knew they had prayed diligently for my recovery and some of them knew the details, but I wanted to talk about my experience when I returned.

I found myself wondering how I would get through this awkward subject. I still don't know if it was the voice of God or the morphine I was using, but a voice inside me said, *Start off your talk with the audience saying the word rectum aloud three times.* It made sense at the time. I figured if I could get everyone to say it a few times, it might desensitize it so they would not cringe every time they heard me say it. Since I was diagnosed with cancer of the rectum, I knew the word would come up a few times. It turned out to be an unusual and effective ice-breaker that I have used repeatedly.

One time after I had talked to nurses in Atlanta, Georgia, at a Hollister event, I met a colon cancer survivor nurse named San Short. A few months later, she called me up to ask me to visit her hometown of Thomaston, Georgia, to speak at a community event. We talked about the upcoming event on the phone, and she wanted me to use my usual opening with a cautionary note.

"These people down here might not understand what you're saying because you speak so fast. You may have to slow it down. I don't want them to miss it."

"You mean I say the word rectum too fast?"

"I think some people may not get what you said."

"How do I say it, and how should it be said?" I asked, while we laughed.

"You say rect'm."

"How would you advise me to say it so they get it?"

"Reeeccttuum."

I'll keep practicing that San, thanks.

Independent

It was three days after my first surgery for the temporary colostomy. I had a nasal gastric tube, a catheter, and various other tubes coming out of my body. I was crabby and in pain, and that was the day the ostomy nurse was going to teach me to put the ostomy pouch on for the first time.

I was twenty-three years old and my mother felt that she needed to be in the room to understand the ins and outs of dealing with an ostomy. I wanted to be independent. It was a private situation, and I felt that I could handle this on my own. My mother and I had a little spiff, because she felt she should be part of it in case I would not be able to do it. I got madder and testier, and she stormed out of the room because of my attitude.

Later, she ran into my surgeon out in the hallway and confronted him. "I thought you said you removed *all* the a—hole from my son!"

I didn't hear about this incident until three weeks after the fact. My girlfriend was walking around the corner at the hospital and overheard my mother talking to the doctor. She thought it was hysterical. The doctor was surprised at first, and then said, "I've got one of them at home too—you can never get rid of those."

When I heard about it, the next day, I asked my mom innocently, "So—they didn't remove all the a—hole?" My mother burst out laughing.

Paul Warning graduated from the University of Wisconsin-Platteville, in May 2006. He's looking forward to making a splash in the real world. From January to mid-March of 2003, Paul had a temporary ileostomy while waiting for takedown surgery of his J-pouch. He credits his family and friends for helping him through his battle with ulcerative colitis. Paul says, "I have learned how strong I am, and I'll strive to help others going through difficult times dealing with IBD. I hope that my quirky humor can help put a smile on someone's face!" Paul likes the outdoors and being active. His prized possession is a 1991 Ford Mustang GT.

Introduce

When I talk to nurses, I do a little educating from the patient's perspective on things. They are often surprised to find out many nurses forget to introduce themselves. It's understandable with all the patients they take care of each week, but we still feel more at ease as patients when our nurses tell us their names. It makes us feel a better connection when they have to stick weird things into our bodies.

Irrigate

It usually takes me an hour a day. I sit on a chair opposite the toilet to irrigate. Things I might do at the same time while I irrigate, often multitasking:

talk on the phone

paint with watercolor

file my nails

read anything

cut out my pouches

polish my nails

listen to the radio

write a thank you note

put on make-up

fix my hair

crossword puzzles

pray

sleep

clean around me as I sit, (empty wastebasket, scrub toilet, floor,
polish chrome, wipe off sink or shower door)

cut my hair

color my hair

tweeze my eyebrows

journal

light candles and watch them melt

listen to the TV

make a to-do list

write bills or do mundane paperwork

It's amazing how much can get accomplished in one hour.

Italy

When I recovered from ileostomy surgery and some rather harsh cancer treatments, I longed to resume traveling. Our friends thought a trip to Italy would be just the ticket to get me back to good health. I wasn't sure if I could physically handle it.

I asked around and heard stories, the kind that people whisper under their breath. One ostomate thought she was doing me a favor by informing me, "We can't travel by plane, you know. Our bags will fill up with air." Someone else warned me about Italian bathrooms. "People like us have a terrible time." I longed to go to Italy. Determined, I signed up for a tour anyway.

The night before we left, I woke up in the middle of the night in a cold sweat. I imagined my bag blowing up on a plane and its contents spewing all over my fellow passengers. More anxiety dreams followed. Next, I imagined myself trapped in an Italian bathroom with an unflushable toilet.

I was a nervous wreck going through international customs. I worried when they opened my suitcase they would announce on the loudspeaker, "We have found some ostomy supplies here," then hold them out for everyone to see.

On take off, my bag seemed to expand slightly because of air pressure and perhaps gas, or was it just a gas I was finally going to Italy? When we were up in the air, I went into the bathroom and burped out the extra gas. I kept my supplies in my carry-on in case my luggage would get lost. In reality, no customs inspector ever questioned their presence. During the ten days we were in Italy, we never encountered one bathroom that didn't work. Even so, it dawned on me that in case we had, it would have been a problem for everyone. My most amazing revelation came when we were on the bus. People around me were concerned that nature would call and they'd be forced to use the port-a-potty on the back of the bus. Not me, I thought smugly. I had complete control. All of a sudden, I was an object of envy instead of pity. I realized, from that moment, an ostomy would not interfere with my life; I could just sit back and enjoy the ride.

Carol Larson, is an ileostomate and author of "When the Trip Changes: a Traveler's Advisory to Colorectal Cancer" and "Positive Options for Colorectal Cancer." Carol was a teacher in Minnesota for twenty-four years and then diagnosed with Stage III Colorectal Cancer in 1999. A past president for the local ostomy chapter, today Carol works part-time at the library and continues to write. She is a wife to David, and they are the parents of three daughters and grandparents to three little ones.

J-Pouch

I had been going to J-Pouch support meetings in Philadelphia. The nurse that ran the meeting gave me a bag to take home to show to my family. Explaining the surgery, I told them I would have a temporary ileostomy where the doctor would bring my intestine out and my waste would go into this bag. "That's the bag?" my daughters Rachel and Rebecca asked. With relief they said, "We thought it was going to be like a Safeway bag."

Ileostomies can sometimes fire off and inflate at will. One day the girls were getting ready for school and the bag took off, as they sometimes do. Matter of factly, Rachel said, "There goes that bag again."

When I first came home from the hospital, the home health care nurse visited me. On the initial visit, they assess not only your physical condition, but your state of mind as well. Tentatively, she asks, "How do you feel about your ileostomy?" I blurted out, "I love it. I know when I go to the bathroom, it's only going to take five minutes, four pieces of toilet paper, and not going to hurt." Anybody that has had acute or chronic ulcerative colitis understands this, because sometimes the cramping was so intense, it made me cry out. I have met women that have had similar pain describe it as worse than childbirth. Being able to go to the bathroom and have it *not* hurt was **wow.**

Dave Hirschhorn of Arlington, Virginia has had ulcerative colitis for over twenty years with a temporary ileostomy before J pouch surgery in November of 2000. He is married to Debbie and they have two children. He has been the webmaster for his ostomy group and chat host and moderator for J-pouch.org. Dave has spoken nationally on J-Pouch and the issues surrounding it. In November of 2004, Dave was diagnosed with ALS (Lou Gehrig's) disease and since then has attended the national patient advocacy days and spoken in front of the senate on Capitol Hill on the urgency of moving along research and drugs for short lived patient communities. He jokes, "I go down hard and loud."

Jet Pack

I have had ulcerative colitis and proctitis since I was ten years old. The disease got worse as I aged and had stressful challenges. When my father was diagnosed with brain cancer in 1998, I took a turn for the worse. In 2003, we lost our business, had marital strife, and my life seemed to be in the toilet, literally and figuratively. I had been nonstop sick for three years when I prayed to understand the point of this illness. God showed me a picture, with my toes curled over the edge of a diving board. He told me I was at a major transition in my life, a letting go of something big, a radical transformation a year from then, in which my life would be unrecognizable. It would free up my emotional, physical, and spiritual energies, and I would propel forward with a jet pack on my back to fulfill my life's purpose.

At that time, my colon was starting to ulcerate, but I wasn't aware of it for months. After spending a month in bed, losing twenty-five pounds in three weeks, I was hospitalized for malnutrition and dehydration weighing in at ninety-five pounds. My colon was collapsing to the point I had almost stopped absorbing all nutrition and hydration. Five days before surgery, I learned I would lose my entire colon and have ileostomy surgery, or I would die.

In my room and at the hospital, I felt held by God and strength came to me by the presence of my deceased father and sister, who I felt were with me in spirit and comforted me the entire time until I left the hospital. I was completely pain-free for thirty minutes one Sunday morning before I was given morphine. I looked at the clock and realized it was the exact time at church when healing prayers were spoken; I had not been pain-free for over three years.

I had to lose my colon to save my life, which helped me to get a life. My ostomy surgery changed everything; I loved to eat for the first time in my adult life—even hospital food tasted fantastic. Buffets gave me the perfect opportunity to taste a wide variety of foods, and I have gained seventy pounds since surgery.

I have traveled to three continents in the last nine months, including trips to Asia, Europe, and India and whale-watched in Mexico. I have gone parasailing, paragliding, exercised, enjoyed the theater, and am glad I never have to have a colonoscopy again. Even my sex life improved since I wasn't in pain anymore.

Having an ostomy is not perfect. I have to deal with the bag in the middle of the night, or change the way I dress to accommodate the bag. I get concerned about acceptance in an intimate situation. Still, it's an incredible gift I wouldn't trade back for a second. It has given me a life, a fabulous life.

Anita Singewald is an ileostomate, living with her two daughters in Minnesota. Her background is in psychology and she plans to start a counseling group for ostomates in the Twin Cities. She likes to garden and make chocolates.

Johnny On the Spot

In May, I walked in a 10 km walkathon for The Bell Telephone Kids Help Line in Canada. We had walked about halfway when I decided to check the pouch. My friend went to get water while I stood in line for the "Johnny on the spot." It's not the greatest washroom, but will do in a pinch. There I stood until it was my turn and finally, I went in. As I went to empty my pouch, I dropped my clip down that dreaded toilet!

I had nothing with me, my purse was locked in the car five kilometers away. I rolled my pouch over and went out to my friend. I told her my problem, and she agreed to leave. We were about to turn around when I remembered what we had received for walking, a pair of shoelaces. Both of us laughing, I hid behind a parked vehicle, she kept watch, and I tied the lace around the bottom of my pouch in a nice tight bow. No one noticed a thing and off we went to complete our walk.

Louise Ward lives in Ontario, Canada, and has had an ileostomy since January 2000 due to severe Crohn's Disease. She works part time and is involved in caring for her father with Alzheimer's disease. She has been married for twenty-five years with children and grand-children always keeping her busy.

Keyhole Locks

I decided, after a diagnosis of cancer, that I wanted to find humor in all situations. The oncologist gave me some great advice when he said, "Live your life without worrying about the cancer." After that perspective, I never thought twice about how I go to the bathroom.

One day, as I was spending time with my three-year-old niece and four-year-old nephew, I needed to use the bath-

room. My niece, being aware of potty training, wanted to follow me into the bathroom. I wouldn't let her come in with me so she proceeded to scream, "I want to watch!" I brought her out to the hall and closed the door. My four-year-old nephew came running up the stairs to see what was wrong. I told him what was bothering his sister.

In my sister's house, they have keyhole locks. I was facing the toilet using my intermittent catheter into my stoma so all that was visible was the stream of urine, which makes me look like I pee like a guy. All of a sudden, I see a four-year-old eyeball into the keyhole and a little voice yelled, "Auntie Karen, why do you have a penis?" So I said to him through the door, "I don't." Cautiously, I opened the door. "It's what the doctor made so that I can go potty."

My sister and I were rolling on the floor laughing. I said to her to be ready when her son goes back to school and tells everybody that his Auntie Karen has a penis. Now whenever I go into the bathroom, they ask me if I am going to use that thing the doctor gave to me.

Karen Bazany, continent urinary diversion-urostomy, as a result of urethral cancer, January 18, 2002. A single woman with a cute Maltese puppy named Sadie, Karen has a large supportive family, with her mom and dad; five brothers and sisters, all with spouses and significant others; and twelve beautiful nieces and nephews. She is a first grade teacher and enjoys scrapbooking, crafts, walking, and travel.

Last Rites and Irish Coffee

I had my original surgery when I was thirty years old in 1975. The ulcerative colitis had gotten progressively worse with no remission in sight. I even had to carry a change of underwear and a plastic bag in my toolbox at work, just in case I'd have an accident. I'd been so sick, a priest had given me last rites. Thirty years ago I had a Kock pouch, but it didn't work, so I had a temporary ileostomy until they could try a Kock pouch again. That wasn't until 1985, but I'm still using it. At the time of surgery I had a total colectomy. The doctor sent me home with a big supply of maternity sanitary napkins.

I had to wear the pads after the surgery while my wound healed. The next week, a friend of mine was going water skiing at Lake Havasu in Arizona and invited my girlfriend and me along since he knew I was home recuperating. They are Japanese and had an exchange student from Japan staying with them.

On the first day, my friend's wife knocked on the door and explained that the exchange student had started her period and needed feminine products. I offered her my extras and she took them. Later, my friend's wife told me the student wanted to thank my girlfriend for the supplies. They didn't want to confuse her about why a man might have sanitary napkins so we went along with it.

Later, I worked for the navy, and I was at an OSHA seminar in San Francisco. One night, we decided to go by bus to find all the places that served Irish coffee. After four hours of drinking Irish coffee, I went into my room, and changed my bag. Instead of emptying it, I unintentionally ripped it all off and flushed it down the toilet. Too many Irish coffees I would say. I sobered up quickly as I saw the last bit of it go down into the toilet. I learned putting on a new pouch when you're plastered is not that easy.

Nick Berger of California is a certified SCUBA Diver, a snow skier, and enjoys river rafting. He works out at the gym three days a week. A few years ago, he remodeled his house, which the local paper ran a two-page article on. He builds and shows exotic cars for a hobby and currently has a 1968 Jag XKE and a 1963 Studebaker Avanti.

Life

We were stationed in Chile with the US navy and were amongst an association of Americans who lived there. Two of the women were former schoolteachers who had retired and lived in Santiago. They had a Scottie dog, which was very ill with symptoms that resembled to me dehydration, nausea, and vomiting. I asked them, "Does your dog like Coca Cola?" "Sure," they said. "Give the dog some coke. He just needs electrolytes," I told them. Within hours, the dog was responding better. They reported a few days later that the dog had fully recovered, and they credited me with saving his life. I would not have known that he needed hydration had I not been an ileostomate.

Barbara Hawes of Chantilly, Virginia, has had an ileostomy since 1962 due to Crohn's Disease. She has been the editor for her ostomy chapter newsletter for many years. She is married to Bill and they have two children, five grandchildren, and are active in church. Barbara works part time as a secretary and enjoys reading in her spare time.

Love Story

I met someone important in my life when I was just fourteen years old. He was one of my brother's best friends, but it was taboo to date your buddy's sister. After I went to college and he to the military, we dated a couple of times and then went our separate ways. Every few years, we would run into each other, go out a few times, exchange contact information, or just say hello, and go back to our busy lives. In 2001, I ran into my old friend James and we started dating again more seriously. While we had been out of touch, he had attended college and became a registered nurse.

Intestinal woes plagued me since birth with problems worsening in my mid-twenties when I would have episodes. I put off going to the doctor and suffered for fifteen years, which I don't recommend.

James and I were engaged, when at age forty, I had a severe episode. He urged me to go to the hospital, but I resisted until 3:30 a.m. when I awoke with the most intense pain I have ever experienced. At the emergency room, the doctor said my large intestine had ruptured and would need surgery. The surgeon arrived, looked over to James and said, "Hey, I know you." James and the surgeon had worked together at one of the largest ERs in Atlanta; I felt better already. The surgeon suspected I had undiagnosed diverticulitis resulting in a perforated colon and that I would probably be fitted during surgery with a temporary colostomy.

By 7:00 a.m. that morning, I was in surgery, where part of my large intestine and a portion of my bladder were removed. I had a tough time in recovery and spent five days in the intensive care unit. I was hooked up to all sorts of beeping machines, a foley catheter, an NG tube, oxygen, IV's and now, a colostomy. It seemed I had something stuck in every orifice and now featured a new one. James entered the room swinging a small plastic bag and proclaimed, "Here's your TED hose." "Where do they stick that?" I asked. He explained they were anti-thrombolitic, support stockings. That's when I decided to name my colostomy TED.

I came home with TED, a Foley catheter, a ten-inch abdominal wound, a yeast infection from the antibiotics, and my period—a head cold was all that was absent.

During the three months with the colostomy, James did two dressing changes daily, and was even pooped on in the middle of the night when the bag failed. Advised to remove the dressing for nightly showers meant that James had to be there to put me back together. He truly knows me from the inside out. I had prayed for affirmation that James was the person I would be with forever. God's answer came in the form of a colostomy. Laughing together got us through those three months.

While recovering, my sister came every day from noon to 6:00 p.m. so I wouldn't be alone. Right before my reconnect surgery, my sister told me she was nine weeks pregnant with her second child. I counted back and informed her she had gotten pregnant at the time I was in ICU. She responded with, "You spend your time the way you want, and I'll spend my time the way I want."

My colostomy was taken down three months later. During both recoveries, I had to ask James and Mom to take care of my basic needs. It was humbling, but we got through it with love and humor.

Nancy Hall from East Point, Georgia, had a temporary colostomy in 2003 due to diverticulitis. She is a finance manager for one of the country's largest health insurers. She loves spending time with James, likes to play the piano a little, and golf a lot.

M

Matches

A friend's brother told me that he controlled his odor by lighting a match in the bathroom. I did this once shortly after having my colostomy fourteen years ago. Thinking I would be smart and get it all before it smelled up the room, I let the air out of the bag and lit the match right next to it and WHOOSH!, my bag had a melted area and my stoma lit up with flame. It scared the heck out of me. What was I thinking? I knew that gas was explosive. I've heard of guys lighting their farts before, so I should have known. Is a woman's gas any less combustible than a man's? No! Moral of the story: Be careful if you use matches.

Lori Samson resides in Newton, Iowa, with her husband, Craig, and two children. She is a lab technician, helped to start the local ostomy support group, and keeps busy with the kids' activities. Lori likes to ride bikes, go on walks, scrapbook, and stamp. At the age of twenty-six, she had surgery for rectal cancer, but she didn't let it slow her down.

Mercedes Benz

There are perks to living rectum-free and being vocal about it. Betsy Naeger, a nurse who worked with the local ostomy support group, called me to come to St. Louis, Missouri, to give a talk at their annual ostomy product fair. She said accommodations would be provided and a limousine would pick me up at the airport. The week before I was supposed to arrive, I called Betsy when I realized I didn't know which hotel I would be staying at. She laughed and said, "Oh, no, we have room in our garage behind the house." This will be a first, I thought, but as long as I had a bed to sleep in and a bathroom to use, what else would I need?

The morning of my talk in Missouri, my father drove me to the airport. We bantered back and forth about my schedule, and I told him that night I would be staying in someone's garage in St. Louis. We both laughed, and he gave me a hard time about how I had made the big time now.

When I stepped off the plane, there was Betsy, holding a sign with my name on it. "The limousine is waiting outside," she said. I played along, thinking it was really going to be a mini van like the one I had at home. Imagine my surprise when her husband pulled up in a 1979, gray Lincoln Town Car limousine, one of many of his vehicles. Leonard is a professor of pharmacology at the St. Louis College of Pharmacy and has a passion for cars. We talked about his car as he drove Betsy back to work at Medical West Healthcare to finish details for the evening gathering.

The two of us continued on and a few miles later, Leonard drove up to the nicest house on the block with a garage that held twelve cars on the bottom floor. Up above the garage was an apartment with a table that sat sixteen comfortably, a large TV, stereo, and a completely stocked kitchen and bath. After Leonard carried my suitcase up to my "room," he suggested we go out to lunch. He asked, "Which car shall we take?" Many of them were under covers and as he lifted one I said, "That will do." It was a vintage 1970 Rolls Royce, white with tan interior. Off we went for a tour around town and the local corner pub for a drink and a sandwich. Leonard was great company and conversation flowed. He asked, "What's your favorite car?" I told him about the time when I was around eighteen, I saw a Mercedes Benz 450 SL for the first time. My father used to tease me because I told him, "Someday, I'm going to have one of those." When he told me how much they cost, I didn't think about it much after that. Leonard asked, "What's your favorite color?" I told him red or blue would be my top choices.

Leonard was a good listener, an intelligent academic, and a real motor head that passed on the passion to his sons. The entire neighborhood enjoyed his hobby because Leonard and his family had a reputation for having fun yearly parties in the garage. It was the kind of place the local cops would drive by, stop in for a soda, and see the latest car the guys were working on.

After lunch, I retreated to my room where I laid down on the bed with the sun shining through the skylight and took a restful nap. A couple of hours passed, and it was time for me to give my talk at the hospital and sign some books. It was a fun night, and I met many great people; a few hours later, we were back in the garage.

Leonard and Betsy brought a bottle of wine; we ate some appetizers and talked as long as we dared, since my plane would depart at sunrise heading on to Texas for a talk that night. Before saying good night, Leonard disappeared and came back a few minutes later to tell me he had a gift to give me. I was touched. It was a red, 1974 Mercedes Benz 450 SL with black interior. My dream car. Okay, it was a Jim Beam collector decanter, but that made it easier to take on the plane. I display it in my office and whenever I look at my Mercedes, I cherish the memory with Leonard and Betsy Naeger and the great welcome into their lives.

Mile High Club

Gil Lorenz of Fenton, Missouri, shared his version of the mile high club. "We were on an airplane heading for Vancouver when all of a sudden, my pants were wet. I grabbed my good old pink tape and headed for the rest room to try to repair my appliance. We were having some turbulent weather. I simply could not fix it. I opened the door and told the flight attendant my problem. I asked. "Would you please ask my wife to come back here?"

What a time we had. The plane was jumping around, and we were both in the bathroom. You know how tiny those rest rooms are on the plane and neither of us are small people. She sat on the toilet seat and I was hanging on to the wash-basin. After about twenty minutes, we got the job done. My wife asked, "What should we say when we leave here?" I said, "Nothing—just smile!"

Gil and Melba Lorenz have been married for sixty-six years, and they have a family of thirty. They are retired and spend their time taking care of each other these days. Gil had a urostomy in 1999 due to cancer.

Mirror

The colorectal surgeon at my hospital asked me to see a particular woman experiencing an enormous amount of anxiety concerning her upcoming ostomy surgery. Wanting to allay the fear that comes so easily with the unknown, I spent the better part of an hour telling her about the surgery, showing her pouching options, and discussing the post-op care of her stoma. Her fears relieved, she proceeded with her colostomy, and, after her surgery, I went to her room for her first pouch change. I found her holding court with her husband and four of their best friends.

After I told her privately what I planned to do, she dismissed the men and begged her girlfriends to stay for the "reveal." As I removed the pouch, she asked her friend to hand her a makeup mirror. With the pouch off, and the stoma cleaned, the patient focused the mirror on her new stoma and exclaimed in an alarmed tone, "It's SO BIG!" After another glance, she then looked up at us sheepishly, chuckled, and announced, "Oh...that was the magnifying side." The humor of the moment and the laugh that we all shared were wonderful for tension relief, and the patient quickly went on to accept and care for her stoma.

Bev Biller, RN, CWOCN, of Sudbury, Massachusetts, received her BSN at Wayne State University in Detroit, Michigan, and moved to Boston in 1977. After a twelve-year hiatus in her nursing career during which she raised four sons, she received her WOCN training at Wicks Educational Associates in Harrisburg, Pennsylvania. Since 1998, she has worked at the New England Medical Center as their WOCN.

Mope

Sure, go ahead and mope for a little while. Having an ostomy can be a bummer. As soon as you can, turn that mope into hope—then you can cope.

Name Tags

My wife, Sue, had an operation for a colostomy in 2003. With all the new changes to her body, she was extremely self-conscious of her clothing. She would always ask, "Can you tell anything?" I would say, "Gee, Sue, it's not like you have a sign around your neck saying you have an ostomy. No one can tell. Relax about it."

Two years later, we were at the United Ostomy Association conference in Anaheim, California. At one time, I looked at Sue and had to laugh. "Sue, remember that conversation we had about not wearing a sign  around your neck saying you have an ostomy?" We both had to laugh when we realized she was wearing a big name tag that said just that: Sue Norby, MN, colostomy.

Paul Norby is husband to Sue, a colorectal and breast cancer survivor. The Norby's have been married since 1981 and have a son, Jacob. Since Sue's surgery, both she and Paul attend two different support groups for colorectal cancer and people living with ostomies. They needed support, and now they have become the ones that share much needed encouragement for new ostomates and cancer survivors. Sue's on a mission to help educate and inform others about colorectal cancer screening too.

Noises

Years ago while I was working with a client, my colostomy suddenly made a lot of noise. It was so noticeable that my client stopped in mid-sentence. She knew my medical history and that I had an ostomy. She looked right at my abdomen, said, "Hey, I'm talking here," and carried on as if nothing abnormal had happened.

Novelty

A couple summers ago, we were visiting relatives at their cabin. My husband, Bob, is a novelty and has always been a source of curiosity for our great nephews and nieces because he is paralyzed from his shoulders down and uses a wheelchair. In 1964, Bob became a C4-5 quadriplegic after getting hurt in a shallow water diving accident. The great nieces and nephews are fascinated by Bob and like to help him.

The bathroom in the cabin is very tiny, and he can't get fully into it with his wheelchair. I have to position him in the doorway (half-way in, half-way out) when I am washing him and brushing his teeth. The kids watch and think its cool. Sometimes we require privacy for toileting needs.

One afternoon, when we didn't think anyone was around, we went in to empty his leg bag, which is strapped to the lower calf of his leg. I lifted his leg up to the toilet and pulled the rubber cap off the bottom of the bag and the urine squirted out into the bowl. Little did we know that one of our little nieces was watching and promptly yelled, "Mom, Mom, Uncle Bob can pee through his leg!"

Penny Peters is a wife to Bob Peters who has been a urostomate since 1981. Bob is involved in disability-related local, state, and national activities that seek to improve the lives of people with disabilities.

Numerous Beers

There was a man in Australia that was rather fond of beer. He'd had a temporary ostomy with no problems adjusting to it and didn't let that stop him from enjoying himself. After numerous beers, he decided the rest of the patrons should share in his surgical adventure, so he proceeded to step onto a table and remove his ostomy pouch. The poor barman, amidst the chaos, saw the stoma and thinking the patron had been stabbed, immediately called an ambulance. The man was rather prominent in the area and stopped drinking after that embarrassment.

Jill Jones has been a nurse for four decades and a enterostomaltherapist for twenty of those years. Married for thirty-six years, she has two children and reporting more grandchildren on the way. She enjoys reading, cooking, sewing, and travel. Some of her travels have taken her to Japan, Singapore, Fiji, New Zealand, and all over her native country of Australia.

Nurse Admiration

Before my husband's urostomy surgery, I took a class from the ET on how to change the pouch. Squeamish around blood, I wasn't sure how I'd handle seeing a real stoma. Everything was in order to change the bag, the alcohol and adhesive wipes and many other pieces were laying on the bed, ready to go to work. I felt confident until I saw the urostomy. When the nurse pulled the sheets back and took off his bandages, it was supposed to be a hands-on experience. Instead, I thought, "Lady, you're the expert."

I started passing out. She took me, shook my arm, and said sternly, "Don't you dare do that. You are the only help he has when he gets home." I saw the stints sticking out that run out of the stoma and the pouch has to be put on carefully. The stints typically hang down in the pouch and thread through the stoma up into the ureters. It is easy to change the pouch when the stints are in there, but once they are out, you have to fight the urine all the time because it's constantly dripping out.

Because of the ET's directness, I snapped out of my fainting spell. I was mad, upset, and felt caught in a situation with no way out. Thank God, she made me face it and stay there. With the ET's experience, she knew what to say, and my hat is off to her.

At first my husband did not want to leave the house, but that changed after we attended a support meeting and met other ostomates. We met a woman there who had just returned from China. He said, "If she can go to China, I can go to Florida." Since then, he has been the president of our local ostomy chapter for over two years; he is on the board of directors and edits our newsletters. I am proud of him.

My husband's cancer reoccurred in the abdomen—the same type of cancer, and it has been the nurses that got us through it all so far. We go to his chemo appointment at seven in the morning. There are thirty chairs lined up for the patients at four shifts a day. The nurses laugh and make jokes all day long to help the patients get through everything. Humor helps the patients a lot, and it's the nurses who keep everybody happy. They are a big part of our healing.

Monie Bordanaro is a caregiver to husband, Lou, who had a urostomy in 2000 for bladder cancer. They have two children and three grandchildren that are the loves of their lives. Monie likes to sew, make porcelain dolls, and collect them. Lou is the president of their local ostomy group. They both like to travel and have fun.

Ode

Ode to a Filter

I like your style, you're so discreet.
With your job well done, I still smell sweet.
Bring on the onions, the sodas, the beans.
I'm no longer worried about causing a scene.

In planes, at games, home, and work,
Flatulence dissipates, oh, what a perk.
Thank you, filter makers, you've made my day,
I go through life in a much happier way.

Brenda Elsagher

Odor

For some people, one of the side effects of ostomy surgery and the adjustment is a constant odor that seems to permeate everything in the beginning. I couldn't seem to get rid of the odor, and I felt like a walking Port-O-Potty. I was complaining about it to just about anyone that would listen. They would offer suggestions: "Are you keeping it clean? Maybe it's all in your mind." I could not believe it because the offending smell was definitely there.

I sought the proper help with medical people and even consulted a health specialist. I woke up smelling it, smelled it all day, and went to bed smelling it. While I was at home recovering, my sister-in-law was caring for me. One day when I got out of the shower, I started complaining about the odor again to her. My brave sister-in-law said, "Let me smell what you are talking about." As she approached me, I opened my sweat pants. She stuck her nose in my pants and sniffed, "I can't smell anything at all." We both laughed hard as I comprehended it *was* in my head, and I realized we knew a lot about each other—maybe too much.

Annette Peterson is a colostomate since 2004, due to Crohn's Disease, and lives in Chicago, Illinois. With a lucrative career as an account manager in the financial industry, she also loves to oil paint and eat. She laughs about the fact she has gained twenty-five pounds since surgery because finally everything agrees with her, except her wardrobe— it has gotten tighter. After surgery, she met a good man, and they look forward to some travels together. Annette joked, "It will be the first time I'll actually be able to use my vacation time for fun instead of doctors and hospital visits. Life is great!"

Old Joke

It's not so bad having a colostomy. I just can't find shoes to match my bag.

Source unknown

Optimists

I was attending a national conference in Las Vegas for the United Ostomy Association and was riding in the elevator with a man who apparently was not part of our conference.

He squinted as he read my name tag and said, "The United Optimists Association?"

"Nope," I said, "The United Ostomy Association."

"What's that?" he asked.

Our doors were just about to open onto our floor when I said, "It's an organization that provides support for people that have ostomies."

"Okay, I give up, what's an ostomy?"

"People with the bags have ostomies—you know, like colostomies, ileostomies, and urostomies."

He suddenly turned red and looked embarrassed. As we were walking off the elevator, I blurted, "Have you heard of that expression, 'When God closes a door, He opens a window?'"

He nodded.

"We have windows," I said. He smiled, and we went on our way.

Outhouse

Having an ostomy made life better because I was sick until I was twelve; I never had the same strength as the other kids. When I was getting sick, I would disguise it from my parents to prevent the trip to the hospital. Sometimes I'd be there for ninety days. My teachers were great even though I missed tremendous amounts of school. My surgery released me from all of that.

I became a mom with an ostomy and have been using Hollister products for forty-two years. I have seen so many good changes through the years. When I was in labor about to have my baby, I changed my appliance. It stayed on through labor, contractions, and an additional two days—a good test for a pouch.

One morning my husband and I were going out fishing. I had to make one last potty stop because he hates to come back once he's on the river. In the state park, I used the outhouse, finished my job, and reached for my clip. Horrified, I watched it go down to the bottom of the outhouse. He heard me screaming, "My clip is gone."

We happened to have a box of key rings in the trunk of my car. One of them fit right over my appliance, and it did not interfere with anything. I just pried it open to empty the pouch and it held beautifully. I caught the first fish and nothing wrecked our day.

Nora Needy of Illinois has been an ileostomate since 1964, diagnosed with ulcerative colitis at age six. She never let her ostomy stop her from having a good time. She's enjoyed camping, traveling, bowling, reading, and hanging out with her daughter, Ginger, and grandson, Aren. She's been a teacher, recently received her Master's degree and has been a member of her local ostomy chapter in Joliet for twenty-eight years.

Pee Pee

My niece was about four years old when I went to visit her family. Soon, it was me and my shadow, with my niece following me everywhere for the two weeks I was there. The first trip I went to the bathroom, I showed her this is how Aunt Mary Jane goes to the bathroom. In an airport with my brother, I took my niece and we went off into the bathroom. In the background, she yelled to my brother, "Did you know Aunt Mary Jane goes pee pee in a bag?"

Mary Jane Wolfe, of Framingham, Massachusetts, has had a urostomy since 1968. A former Sam Dubin Award winner, FOW (Friends of Ostomates Worldwide) board member, and Youth Rally volunteer for UOA, she has been instrumental in helping ostomates of all ages.

Peek

When patients I need to work with are waking up from surgery and they have not met me, I walk in the room, introduce myself and say, "I'm your new best friend. I'm Jan, your ET nurse, and I'm going to peek under the covers." They usually wake up instantly.

Jan Clark, CWOCN, for eleven years with a practice from neonates to the elderly. She is a lover of jazz and spends time between her San Antonio home and her beach cottage.

Photos

I was getting ready to go on a TV show, and the woman touching up my makeup relayed the following story about her husband. He was just arriving for his first colonoscopy. As he walked into the doctor's office to prepare for the test, he noticed photos of various colons hanging on the wall. When the doctor came in my husband asked, "Do you recognize anyone by their faces anymore?"

Polo Shirt

After nearly thirty years of brutal colitis, my colon was removed. I ended up with an ileo-rectal pull-through after nearly a year of having an ileostomy. There were speed bumps along the way, a surprise cancer tumor that broke through the colon wall, the six months of chemo, a large blood clot near my liver, a rare liver disease, and numerous life threatening blockages. I also feared knowing that at any moment I could need a permanent ileostomy or that the cancer might return.

I called up to order ostomy products over the phone and felt judged. I was not really one of *those* ostomy people; mine was only temporary. The status of temporary and permanent got muddier as I began to realize that the ileostomy was irrelevant, other than the physical management and workings. I began to seize control of my own insecurities I had projected out into the world.

Writing my song "Pooped" helped me "out" myself to conquer my own vanity. I met people and immediately told them about my bag and asked if they wanted to see it; only half were curious. The only baggage I was carrying was literal; it was a relief to stop hiding. I thought I had conquered my ego when I went to perform my songs at the United Ostomy Association national conference in Anaheim, California, in 2005.

Internally I referred to my audience as *them*. I was not one of *them*, I was doing *them* a favor. Conversations with participants revealed similar stories to mine and that was scary. Here, I wouldn't get the typical dinner party pity I had grown accustomed to receiving, their stories of suffering often topped mine. In common spirit, I wore my UOA placard around the hotel so strangers could recognize me as the singer guy. One time, I noticed nonmembers peeking at the placard to see what group it identified. I quickly flipped it around to avoid discovery.

I was hiding from strangers, and I didn't even have an ileostomy anymore. It was my ego. It had returned and had grown larger than ever and had shrouded itself beneath the charitable work I had been doing. It made me sick to see how much control the eyes of strangers wielded over my happiness. I noticed a few other ostomates with their flipped placards, and I felt sad. I turned my card back to the readable position and wore it all around the hotel. It stung and felt weird, but I wore it defiantly and proudly. I only challenged myself as no one was hassling me or outwardly judging me. I walked out to the Disney tram to go to meet my family and began to take the placard off. Internal dialogue followed. *Why am I taking this off? I am not wearing this to Disneyland—that would be humiliating. Perfect, that's just what I need.* I wore that placard from ride to ride all day and all night until it no longer embarrassed me.

Bret Martin had a temporary ileostomy. He is a singer and songwriter and is happily married to Holly. They live in northern California and stay busy taking care of their four children. Bret has a hobby of taking long baths (and he does look very clean close up).

Pooped on my Polo Shirt
Lyrics by Bret Martin

I went to visit Randal at his house to work on some songs
   for a play.
His doggy jumped on me like I was salami, and he snagged
   my poop bag clip away.
I juggled and struggled and snapped it back on protecting
   my pandora's pouch,

Then that dog followed me with curiosity and joined me
    on his master's couch.
He nuzzled my belly because it was smelly, never bothered
    to sniff my behind.
What kind of creature has this unique feature? It's enough
    to blow a little dog's mind.
I nearly pooped on my polo, pooped my polo, poopooed
    my polo shirt;
Thank God I averted and nothing had squirted, no poop
    on my polo shirt.
Next time I'll take a little bit, a kibble, put it in my back
    pocket,
Right here, doggy, sniff and nibble,
Have at my butt, just lay off my bag, now stop it, stop it.
I drove home that evening, at least now I had a good story
    to share with my friends.
That same night they came over I told them 'bout Rover;
    we all laughed together and then
I got up to gorge myself, on chocolate cheesecake mousse,
Then things all went to hell. Oh, Miss Manners, what
    should I do?
I pooped on my polo shirt, spoiling all thoughts of dessert.
    It just burst out my bag,
Oh, man, what a drag, I poopooed my polo shirt,
Also soiled my panties, made tacky my khakis, then on to
    my socks it did spurt.
Rolled off my shoe, oh what could I do? I sure hope that
    Stainmaster works.
I'll double clip, that's what I'll do,
    not to mention strategic duct tape.
I'm like a monkey at the zoo, flingin' doo doo hopping on
    one leg,
Popped my piñata, fertilized the floor; yeah, pooped on my
    polo shirt.
Our carpet was spotted, my ileum knotted, how could this
    get any worse?

No kids, look out, don't do it—too late, they ran through it.
While my wife's scrubbing down on her knees, I looked at
  my friend wondrin' *will*
this ever end? He said s—t happens, and I'm inclined to agree.

*You can hear this song at: http://www.cancercrooner.com. Bret
Martin received a standing ovation after singing this song in front of
several hundred people living with ostomies.*

Popcorn

I was in the hospital, and the inevitable time came several days after surgery when there was actual stool in the pouch; I pushed the call button. Morphine made me think I was hilarious.

I thought I was being funny when I said, "Elvis has left the building." "What?" was the response.

Resigned, I said, "There's stuff in my bag."

"Oh, I'll be right down," was the quick reply.

I started apologizing to the nurse about her being stuck with this task.

"I used to change pouches all the time until they trained in nurses that are called ETs or WOCs that specialize in this area. I rarely change an appliance anymore, but I don't mind doing it at all."

"I can't imagine someone would choose this for a profession."

Trying to make me feel more at ease, the nurse said, "They do, and they are good at it. They get so comfortable with the whole process, I bet they could eat popcorn with one hand and change a pouch with the other."

Pregnant Pleasure

In January 2003, I was thirty-two years old and forced to make a decision to have ostomy surgery that ultimately saved my life. I was feeling well after ostomy surgery and soon experienced what I considered a minor flare-up of Crohn's Disease—nothing I couldn't manage with good food, some stress management, and much needed rest. My boyfriend remained by my side through it all, and two weeks before my operation, he proposed marriage. Six months later, we were married.

My colon rectal surgeon advised me to wait a year before getting pregnant so that my body could heal. I started taking prenatal vitamins in January 2004, in preparation to conceive. Months later, we were ready to start a family. We sought out a doctor that had experience in delivering babies to women with both Crohn's Disease and ostomies. He was very patient and answered all of my questions. "Is there anything specifically I should do?" "Keep taking the prenatal vitamins, go home, and get busy. You have to be patient because your uterus is tipped and, due to previous surgeries, you have a lot of scar tissue. It may take a while to get pregnant because of your medical history." He wanted me to be patient and not get discouraged.

On my way home, I got an ovulation kit and pregnancy test. When my husband got home from work, I insisted we get right down to business. We didn't waste much time; two months later I was pregnant.

It wasn't long before the Crohn's Disease started flaring up again. Only now, the flare-ups lasted two to three weeks and were severe. I had horrible fatigue and pain from ulcerations. I had trouble eating and drinking. I went to see my gastroenterologist at the beginning of November 2004, for the first time since my ostomy surgery. I had ulcers in my mouth, throat, and nose; red bumps on my legs; and felt more tired than I thought possible. Even driving home from a long day at the office, I could barely stay awake.

The doctor prescribed a medication to help keep the Crohn's under control. Unfortunately, I had to change after a week because it would not dissolve before passing through my system. Several weeks went by without much progress toward feeling better. At my next doctor's appointment, I was in tears because my Crohn's had gotten so painful. We discussed in detail the issues I had, and I expressed my concerns about my health and that of the baby. My demanding job, the additional stress to my body from my pregnancy was more than I could handle, both physically and emotionally. The doctor told me it was in the best interest of my health for me to stay off work until after the baby arrived.

After a few weeks at home, I started to feel better. Because I had enough rest, watched my diet, and kept my stress low, the Crohn's became manageable. I listened to my doctor. When I felt a flare-up starting, I did very little and rested as much as possible, which helped the remainder of my pregnancy.

While the baby developed, so did a hernia. My abdominal muscles were already weakened by two prior surgeries, and the fact I was sick during my entire pregnancy probably didn't help. A mere sneeze or cough could have caused it while my stomach grew. Concerned about the remote chance of my stoma protruding because of pushing the baby out via vaginal delivery, we decided to have a cesarean section. At the end of my long nine months, I delivered a healthy baby boy—Frankie. I had no complications and was awake for his miraculous birth.

At the UOA national conference months earlier, I attended a session on pregnancy. I had concerns about my stoma extending during pregnancy and not going back down to its normal size. I also worried about increased gas. The speakers assured me that the stoma would enlarge but then go back to normal as I healed. Much to my surprise, my stoma size didn't change at all nor was the gas noise more frequent. The fact I changed my appliance twice a week versus once a week was the only difference I experienced with my ostomy. I had no accidents or leaks either.

Ileostomy surgery has changed my life; I feel better than I have in seventeen years. I can do anything I desire with no limitations. Before surgery, I never would have attempted traveling, especially to foreign destinations. I am active in my community, church, and am the vice president of my local ostomy support group. Blessed with a wonderful family and friends, I have felt their unconditional love. Most importantly, I am the mommy of a healthy, happy baby boy who is the absolute light of my life. I am living proof that ostomy surgery is not the end of the world but the beginning of a new and exciting chapter in the book of life. Looking back, I would not change a thing!

Kathy DiPonio was diagnosed with Crohn's Disease in 1989, at the age of eighteen. She had most of her colon removed in November 1994 when she was twenty-four years old. For several years the Crohn's Disease was active and in full force with little response to medications. Hospitalized several times over the years due to severe flare-ups, in January 2003, she had further surgery to have her colon, rectum, and sphincter muscle removed. She lives in Michigan with her husband and son.

Pure Will

As a statistician and student manager of the basketball team at William Jewell College, Alan Peel was a busy young man. They were near the end of a tournament when he started feeling a blocking sensation around his stoma. He ended up in the hospital with projectile vomiting and a blood pressure of eighty over forty. He had peristomal skin issues that had abscessed requiring emergency surgery. Alan developed sepsis and had a partially collapsed lung, spending the next twenty days in the hospital.

Frustrated by the fact this was his final semester of his senior year, he didn't want to miss any more school. He'd already missed a year in the past that had slowed him down. He willed himself to walk. Even though it was difficult to get to class, he slowly regained his strength, and worked once again with the basketball team as they went all the way to the NAIA Division II Men's National Basketball Tournament.

Tasting the nearness of completing school, he was driven to ace his tests, and it was reflected by his name on the dean's list. The strength, determination, and pure will to get better was punctuated by his walk across the stage that May when he received his diploma. Congratulations Alan!

Alan Peel of Kansas, has been an ileostomate due to Crohn's Disease since May 2003. He has had three surgeries related to the disease—the removal of an abscess and the other being a revision. Currently, Alan is completing his Master's degree in education at Rockhurst University in Kansas City, Missouri.

Privates

While being transported from recovery after surgery, I overheard the nurse yell down the corridor, "Are your privates clean?" It took me a second to realize she was talking about the hospital rooms.

Promise

Promise me you'll learn from my mistake. Never release gas from your pouch in an elevator just because you're alone. People get in on the next floor, and they make embarrassing comments like, "It smells like a dead animal in here." It's hard to hide that kind of guilt.

Pup

There had been a severe tornado in Kansas, and I was at a home spending several hours cleaning debris. The door of the bathroom had been blown away, but I needed to use the facilities anyway. I was emptying my pouch when my clip fell to the floor.

Suddenly, a little pup came out of nowhere, picked up my clip and ran out of the bathroom. There I stood yelling, "He took my clip! He took my clip!" Thank God, there was another woman waiting in the next room. She wrestled the clip from the pup's mouth and returned it to me. I have since learned to carry an extra clip in my pants; you never know when a puppy may appear.

Frances Walters had surgery in 1993 for familial polyposis. Several of her family members had died of it by age thirty-five, so she feels grateful to be seventy-four years old and still enjoying life. She works part time at a florist shop and keeps busy volunteering with the developmentally disabled, cooking, and serving at a food kitchen. She loves to travel and garden.

Quickly

I started being ill at the age of two years old and never knew what it was like to feel healthy. I had ulcerative colitis for sixteen years before surgery. I thought my life was over once I got the ileostomy. Instead, I found out just the opposite.

I am a softball player and have played for twenty-five years. I happened to be playing the field on second base. There was a man on first, when the next player hit the ball to third base. The third baseman turned to throw to me at second, and I tried to force the runner out at second.

Covering second base, I quickly turned to throw to first for the double play. He was already sliding into second base with his spikes standing up at waist high, right into my pouch. I was knocked down to the ground, and within seconds, my pouch contents oozed through my jersey and baseball pants.

At the time, my physician was our center fielder. He saw the entire play and raced in from center field, knowing exactly what had happened. He started screaming, "He's bleeding, he's bleeding. Let's carry him to the car and get him some help." He knew it was not blood. They carried me to my car, the doctor says, "Okay, I'll take it from here. You guys go out on to the field. My doctor then turns to me and then he says, "You do have another change in the car, right?" I nodded yes. "Then change it and get that stupid thing and your butt back out on the field." I changed the pouch and everybody thought that I had gotten a bad gash and was a tough guy. After all, the game must go on.

Dave Rudzin, of Illinois, is a financial analyst and an avid sportsman. Dave loves to make people laugh and always tries to help others. He feels that having an ostomy has taught him valuable lessons in life, and he doesn't accept the word CAN'T. His philosophy is, "If you like what you see, stick around and get to know me better. If not, get the hell out of my way."

Rear Admiral

An affectionate term for gastroentologist or ostomy surgeon.

Rectum

Rectum—darn near killed 'em. *Have you heard that joke a million times too?*

Red Socks

I am the luckiest guy in the world. In 1989, I went for an annual physical and had no symptoms of colon cancer. During the digital rectal exam, the doctor felt a tumor that led to biopsies. Being diagnosed with cancer and finding out that I needed a colostomy was a shock. I realize how fortunate I was that the cancer hadn't spread and was contained.

An ostomate talked with me when I was going through everything. He joked with me, telling me the only thing he couldn't do after surgery was wear a Speedo swimming suit. Well, I never would have worn one anyway.

At the time of my surgery, I was the chief financial officer for Universal Hospital Services, Inc. Our company is in the health care business and we provide medical equipment to hospital and health care providers. I was officially out of the office ten weeks but I had good, capable people filling in for me. After recovering from surgery and the early stages of radiation treatment, I was getting tired. After a while, with the love and support of family and friends around me, I felt better, and, in 1998, I became the president and CEO. Later on, I became chairman of the board.

Back twenty-five years ago, I was a normal businessman, wearing typical business attire. I had the usual collections of black, brown, and navy blue socks, and one pair of red socks. I played golf and used those red socks to feel extra lucky. One morning, in the dark, I grabbed the red socks along with my navy blue suit. It was an important day at work, and our huge deal went through. My friends teased me that I had better wear my red socks more often. I started bringing those socks out for everybody's birthdays at the office. Then people noticed I was wearing them more often on all kinds of joyful events and holidays.

When I was home recovering from surgery, chemo, and radiation, I realized there is more than one day a month that is a special day. Every day is a great day and a spectacular occasion. If you looked in my closet now, you would find twenty-five pairs of red socks and maybe one pair of black. For me it is my daily reminder to myself to find the beauty and wonder of each day. It is great to be alive!

Dave Dovenberg and his wife of thirty-five years reside in Plymouth, Minnesota. Living with a colostomy since 1989, Dave has traveled the world, including wilderness fishing trips in Canada. In his spare time, he enjoys golfing and reading spy novels.

References

While I had been working as a cashier in a store I observed a young coworker in his mid twenties who appeared to have gastric problems. He used Tums constantly, and people at work teased him because he was in the bathroom for long lengths of time. I urged him to see a doctor because his pain caused him to double over. Concerned because of my background with Crohn's, I shared a little bit about my medical history. "I have a bag in the front and the only way the gas comes out is if I release it." I thought he would be comforted that I understood his problems, and I expected he'd keep that information to himself.

One day in the lunchroom, five male coworkers blasted him about hogging the bathroom. I said, "You shouldn't ride him; it's not good when you have stomach problems." Suddenly he burst out with, "Debbie doesn't have regular gas. Hers goes into a bag that she can release when she wants." Conversation ceased, and they stared at me. If they didn't know before that moment, they sure did now. When people learn I don't have a colon they ask, "How do you exist?" I tell them, "I have a bypass and it's called an ostomy." Now that everyone at work knows, I occasionally tease them, "If you don't cover for me, there will be a mess on the floor." They pay attention now.

I offer computer support on the side and teach people how to use computers. An older lady needed help and wanted someone to come to her home. Her daughter insisted on references first, and I listed that I was on the board and the webmaster of our Ostomy Association of Boston. She said, "You're that Debbie? I've talked to you before on the phone. I have an ostomy too." The first time I went to her home, she showed me her little red badge of courage. She was in her eighties and nothing stopped her; that is how I always hope to be.

Debra Florio, a four-year ileostomate, likes to go to casinos and shop. Coincidentally, her husband has ulcerative colitis with a conti-

nent procedure. They met long before either of them understood the ramifications of IBD and have been a good source of comfort and information for each other.

Rookie

After losing a three-year battle with ulcerative colitis in 1955, I had ileostomy surgery at age seventeen. I didn't let that stop me from dating, playing baseball, or other sports, and even went on to play semi-pro ball.

At the time of my surgery the doctor cautioned, "You are going to have to take a desk job. You can't do hard labor now; don't work too much." I thought the hell with that. I began doing things I had done before, and it worked out. Two months after surgery, I shot a deer and dragged it out of the woods.

I graduated high school from a small town in Wisconsin. Soon after that, I worked at the university hospital as an orderly and never came across a patient that had an ileostomy. When I moved to Minneapolis and went into x-ray training, I tore around as a young man would and never let my ostomy stop me. In 1962, I married my wife, and we have two daughters and five grandchildren. I played ball until I was forty-nine and then switched to golf with an eighteen-hole course that I walk.

One time in the hospital, the doctor sent me to visit someone that really didn't want the surgery. "I don't want to be a damn freak," the patient complained to me. "Do I look like a damn freak?" "You have one?" he asked incredulously. He had the surgery.

Another patient came to the department several times. I x-rayed him and felt a bag on the side. I asked him, "Do you have an ileostomy?" "For ten years," was his reply. "I've had mine for thirty-five years. You're a rookie." After that he'd call me the old timer, and I'd call him the rookie even though he was fifteen years older than me.

I would have died if surgery hadn't been an option. I was 6'3" tall and weighed 145 pounds. After surgery, I weighed 117 pounds. Within four weeks, I was back up to 145. A few months later, I was up to 175 pounds and slowly gained weight. Now I feel comfortable at 250 pounds. I have been fortunate to have never required further surgery. I've had a few blockages and needed to go into the hospital when I got dehydrated, but overall, I have had a good life with few ostomy problems.

My friend at the hospital had to have ostomy surgery for ulcerative colitis, and she was unaware I had one. The gastroentologist asked me to visit her. "I hear you are going to have surgery," I said as I entered the room. "I'm not very happy about it," she retorted. Right then I decided to unzip my pants, pull my underwear down and show her my ostomy. "See, it's not so bad." She stared at me and said, "You have one?" Soon the questions started about caring for it, food, sex, and all the rest. I liked helping her see she will get through it. I have had my ostomy for fifty years now, and it hasn't stopped me from doing anything.

David Anderson of Eden Prairie, Minnesota, retired after forty-two years in radiology. After living in their home for thirty-two years, he and his wife traded it in for a condo and help out with that association. In his spare time, David is making cards using his own photography skills.

Round

The desired shape of a stoma voiced by nurses. Patients have no idea at first why it is important. Doctors try to achieve this in most cases. It's way better than rectangular.

Sarcasm

A coping mechanism to help deal with nasty things and moronic people.

Scope

My father recently had his first full colonoscopy, and I had given him a hard time. After I was diagnosed with colorectal cancer and ended up with a colostomy ten years ago, I was surprised he hadn't gotten one earlier. I had lectured my family of ten about the importance of being tested. Several of them had pre-cancerous polyps; I was glad he was following through.

As he prepared for his exam the night before, he jokingly called to let me know "everything was coming out all right. The most difficult part of the preparation is going without solid food for two days."

The doctor put the scope in explaining how his colon looked, and Dad thought the exam was going smoothly until there was a slight snag. The doctor sheepishly admitted, "Your colon is longer than my scope."

My father teasingly replied, "If I see you pulling that thing out and come toward the other end, I'm outta here!"

SCUBA

I looked over at my dive buddy, Mike Ster, and gave him the thumbs up signal. He nodded in agreement, and we began our slow ascent to the surface, pausing occasionally to examine the fossils embedded in the cavern walls. I shined my light at a circular pattern in the limestone. It was a fossilized crinoid, a creature that had lived thousands of years ago after the last Ice Age. Mike flashed his light on several more fossils nearby as we continued upwards towards the surface of the spring.

Paradise Spring is one of hundreds of sinkholes in northern Florida. They are places where the underground aquifer is so close to the earth's surface that the ceiling has fallen in, creating a small open basin filled with crystal clear water from deep within the earth. Most of the springs are connected to a vast underground cave system. Technical divers come from around the world to explore Florida's underwater caverns and caves. Paradise is one of several Florida springs deemed safe for recreational scuba divers like Mike and me.

We stopped our ascent for a few minutes at fifteen feet deep to give our bodies time to get rid of the excess nitrogen we had acquired from breathing air from our scuba tanks while one hundred feet deep in the spring. As we waited, my mind wandered back to 2004.

I was lying in a hospital room in constant pain from the Crohn's Disease that was ravaging my colon. Unlike most Crohn's patients, I did not have to suffer for years before reaching this point. I went from perfectly healthy to facing life as an ileostomate in a matter of months. My husband, Jim, and my family were incredibly supportive, but it was overwhelming for me.

That's when Mike Ster stepped in. Jim and I had become good friends with Mike and his wife, Nancy, in the years since he had taught us to scuba dive. We were vaguely aware that he had a urostomy, but it didn't seem to affect anything he wanted to do, so we rarely gave it a thought. We knew he'd witnessed the atomic bomb tests at Bikini Atoll during WWII and many years later lost his bladder to cancer as a result of the radiation exposure. But far more interesting to us were the stories he told about his exploits in the navy—life on a submarine and learning to breathe underwater using a brand new, technology called Self-Contained Underwater Breathing Apparatus, or SCUBA, for short.

Mike was an inspiration to me during my recovery. He ordered ostomy catalogs and samples, explained how everything worked and even called every few days to see how I was getting along with my bag. Because of the example he set, it didn't occur to me that I should give up scuba diving or limit my activities in any way because of the ileostomy. Mike had already tried many different ostomy appliances, so he knew from experience which brands were "really waterproof and which ones just say they are."

It saved me weeks of trial and error. His practical advice and willingness to answer questions gave me the confidence to take the plunge back into diving after my surgery. My ostomy nurse was amazed at how well I was getting along and how quickly I was able to become comfortable with my situation. I had to give the credit to Mike.

My reflections were interrupted by Mike's signal that it was time to surface. A few minutes later, I was recording another enjoyable dive in my logbook and sharing the experience with other dive friends.

My friendship with Mike has shown me that having an ostomy doesn't prevent me from doing what I enjoy so much, it actually makes it possible. Before the surgery, my physical activities had come to a halt, and I was in no condition to do much of anything. With support and guidance from Mike, my family, and medical team, I have learned to manage my chronic disease and have continued to enjoy my regular activities with very few modifications.

Carol Haack, of Iowa, has had her ileostomy for two years due to Crohn's Disease. An accountant, and part-time PADI divemaster, Carol also likes to wilderness camp and canoe. She and her husband, Jim, make several dive trips each year to Florida, Central America, and the Caribbean.

Sex

Because I was thirty-nine years old when I was diagnosed with cancer and only had been married for six years, I was hugely concerned about sex. After learning I would need a permanent colostomy, a total hysterectomy and would require that part of my vagina be removed and reconstructed, the doctor listened as I expressed concerns about making love with my husband. He offered to connect me with a woman who'd had the same exact surgery as me. "How long ago?" I asked him. "Eleven years ago, but it was a complete success," he added. "How many of these types of surgery have you done?" "You would be my second. Fortunately there aren't a lot of calls for this surgery," he said.

I was excited to talk to the woman he had operated on and within two days I called her. She was in her late sixties when she had the operation and everything went smoothly. We made small talk for a while and then I asked her shyly, "How was your sex life?" "It was good for about six years," she admitted. "What happened then?" I asked anxiously. "Oh, my husband died."

It helped to know that things could work out after surgery, and I felt comforted by talking with her. My husband always wants me to make sure I tell everyone that everything turned out all right. Wink. Wink.

Soil

I've only had one major accident away from home since I've had my ostomy. On my way to visit a friend, I noticed my bag was filling up. I figured I'd just empty it when I got to her place, but decided to release some gas before walking up to the house. As I stood up to get out of my car, having a plant in one hand and a bag of muffins in the other, I felt a warm gush run down my leg. I knew it could only be one thing. My friend was already on her porch starting to come down to greet me when she could tell something was wrong. She knew about my ostomy, and I simply said that I had soiled myself. She immediately said she'd run in to get a paper towel, but I knew it was going to take much more than that to fix the problem. When she came back and saw the brown mess all over my light colored pants, she said, "Oh, when I heard you say 'soil,' I assumed you had gotten a little soil on your pants from the plant. I wasn't thinking you meant this kind of soil."

Up until this point I was almost on the verge of tears standing out on the street covered by my stool. But at that moment, knowing that I was with someone who both cared for me and had a good sense of humor, I just started laughing. She began laughing, too, and invited me in. She suggested that we use her washing machine to clean my clothes and offered her shower facilities as well. During the time we were waiting for my clothes to finish washing and drying, the only thing she had for me to wear was one of her robes—with a leopard skin design! So there we were sitting in her living room talking and laughing about what had happened while I'm wearing this leopard-skin, woman's robe! Of course, I was extremely fortunate that this incident happened with someone like her. But I also learned that by not taking everything so seriously,

I can step outside of myself and see the humor. This had the potential to be a nightmare, but by just shifting my attitude, it turned into something hilarious.

Used with permission from "Straight From The Gut: Living With Crohn's Disease & Ulcerative Colitis" by Cliff Kalibjian

Sprinkler

Jeanne Webber gave me a little peek at her legendary tattoo. There on her abdomen, everything she'd had removed surgically, she had tattooed back on, a complete, colorful colon hung there in all its glory.

A mixture of softness and edginess to her personality, Jeanne has taken a tragic time and mocked it for her own amusement. She relays a story from school when she was in the middle of premedical exams. "The bag was new, midterms were here, and I was nervous and had lots of anxiety. Still awkward with putting the clips on the bag, I accidentally dropped the clip in the toilet. Before I realized what happened, it was gone. I had a big red book that told me all sorts of things to do with lots of information, but it never said be careful about flushing your clip down. I had extra bags, but I did not know what to do. In a hurry, I searched around for something to use.

"The library was nearby, and I found a stapler. Quickly going back to the bathroom, I stapled thirty or forty times until the stapler was empty. I felt confident that it would work. Soon after, a noticeable smell rose from the library and marks started to show up on my jeans. Going back to the bathroom, a friend came along to help me. As I pulled away my clothes, she stood back as I became a human sprinkler.

Luckily, I got an extension to take my chemistry exam later; that was enough biological chemistry for that day."

Later in the year, we had a chance to work on cadavers, a very good opportunity for premed students. I gave my patient an ostomy, made a stoma, and put on a pouch, too, so the whole class could understand ostomy better.

Jeanne Webber-Al-Ghamdi, married to Adel, has had an ileostomy due to ulcerative colitis since Christmas Day 1995. Health problems still linger, but when she is feeling better, you'll find Jeanne at the gym, surfing the ocean, crafting paper art, hiking outdoors, gardening, or playing with her cats.

Standard Operating Procedure

There is no standard operating procedure to tell you how much you should share about your ostomy surgery. Some people keep it very private, while others reveal all. That is an individual decision.

Stoma Names

Mrs. Doris and I met because she needed a urostomy due to bladder cancer. Completely freaked out, she was scared to look at or touch her urostomy. She flat out refused to even attempt to learn how to change or drain the pouch.

After weeks of battling back and forth, her family members exhausted from having to do her care, we agreed to force her to face her urostomy in case of an emergency when no one was available. She reluctantly accepted the concept, but she was still scared to touch the stoma.

As her ET nurse, I wanted to encourage her to learn and be less scared. I placed her chair in front of a mirror and asked her to look at her gums and then touch them. She looked at me as if I had lost my marbles, laughed, and then touched her gums. I asked if that freaked her out to which she said, "Of course not."

Then I took her hands, together we removed the pouch and after cleaning the stoma, I explained that it had no feelings and it was the same tissue as her gums and asked her to touch it. Cautiously, she touched the stoma, realized I was telling the truth, and started to laugh, relieved from her anxiety and fear. I suggested she make up a name for her stoma to personalize her new body part. Without hesitation she told me she would call it "Victor," her husband's name, as her husband and the urostomy were peeing about the same amount all the time. It took time to get her independent, and she finally ended up being in charge of her own care until she passed away from natural causes.

Michael, a cute little red-haired boy was only five years old when he got his permanent ileostomy related to familial polyposis. At the same time, he was in the hospital due to a heart problem. Michael was full of life and, in spite of lacking energy, he was very involved in his own care. At first he hated his new body part. With his sensitive skin, every pouch change was an ordeal with Michael crying and screaming—showing his true red-haired temper.

I wanted to make Michael feel special and look at his stoma with positive eyes. I bought him a cuddly teddy bear, made a stoma of red felt, and sewed it onto the teddy bear's stomach. Next, I placed the same pouch type Michael was using over it and gave Michael the teddy bear.

Michael almost felt sorry for the teddy bear, but he practiced changing the teddy bear's pouch. Little by little, he got more involved in his own pouch changes. As a final attempt to make Michael feel his stoma was part of him, I asked him to find a name for his new friend, his stoma.

After a couple of days of thinking, Michael came up with the name "Fido" as he liked the cartoon character. So from that day on "Fido" and Michael became buddies, and he changed his own pouch with his mom at his side.

Michael was the cutest little guy I have ever met in my entire nursing career. I will never forget him, and I often wonder how he might be doing today, twenty-five years later.

Anne Marie Knudson, ET, San Pedro, California, got her compassion from her father, a teacher and principal at a deaf school in Denmark. She learned sign language quickly because all her playmates were deaf. Her godfather was the principal for a blind school, so working with challenged people and ostomates was a natural fit for her. She gets great joy from her two golden retrievers that share her love of helping others by doing pet therapy at a nursing home: Anne Marie likes hiking, dancing, and writing poetry. A two-time cancer survivor, she has had her share of sorrow, but says that she is still high on life and that she looks for the best in each day.

Supportive

It's ideal when you are fortunate enough to have a large support network. You know you have a supportive spouse when he allows you to publish a book that divulges many of your personal experiences together.

Tampon

I had a urostomy because of bladder cancer. The bladder cancer was serious and complications of surgery turned the operation into a fourteen-hour nightmare that left the surgeons exhausted with results of a poorly placed stoma at the end of a deeply indented appendix scar. They told me it could be repaired but it would be several months before they could reevaluate the condition.

I am an active person involved in water sports such as swimming, scuba diving, sitting in hot tubs, working out, and sweating; watching TV has never been a high priority. I forced myself to be inactive until they removed the stints, but the problem stoma persisted. The pouches would stay on six to eight hours and then I would get that warm, wet feeling that signaled time for a pouch change. I would then cut adhesive strips to fill in the appendix scar and get my skin dry for another application of a wafer and pouch. Everyone told me I had to be patient and that things would get better. Running out of sick time at work, I was having visions of meals delivered to my bathroom. Sleeping on a plastic sheet left a lot to be desired, let alone having quality time with my wife.

The stomal therapist suggested products that didn't work and I called hospitals in Chicago, Minnesota, and anywhere there was an ostomy department and got no useful answers. I finally talked to a radiologist in Wisconsin who gave me words of wisdom I will cherish for the rest of my life. He said, "If you want an honest second opinion you must get out of your geographic area because the doctors and hospitals in one area stick together and communicate with each other."

After a month of my life screwed up, sleep deprivation, and having my wife standing by to give me a third and fourth hand, I found specialists in urology in Dallas, Texas. I couldn't fly because I didn't trust the pouches in a confined area and I didn't want to soil a rental car. My wife and I started out on a cold, cloudy day in March to drive to Dallas. The first day was uneventful and we got to a motel before the dam broke. I had pads placed over the pouch in the event of a disaster.

The second day it was raining, damp, and cold. We stopped to get gas and have a cup of coffee. As I walked to the restaurant, that familiar feeling came on and I told my wife we couldn't go in. It was the middle of the afternoon with no motel in sight. We drove to the far end of the truck stop to get some privacy to replace the pouch. This isn't what I had envisioned doing in the back seat of a car with my clothes partially removed.

My wife and I had considerable practice doing this procedure in a warm dry bedroom with the assistance of a hair dryer to keep the skin around the stoma dry. It was another matter trying to maneuver in the back seat of a car with both of us dripping wet. We got the paper towels out, the skin prep and all the other stuff necessary for the change. This procedure usually took about ten to fifteen minutes. That day it was cold and damp and I was shivering with my pants pulled down around my knees and my shirt pulled up. I was holding a tampon over the stoma through the hole in the wafer so my wife could dry the skin and apply the skin prep and the adhesive filler strips. I was concentrating on what my wife was doing and shaking like a puppy passing a peach seed, and I didn't realize I had inserted the tampon in the stoma. When the wafer was in place and the cardboard applicator removed there was a string sticking out of the stoma. My wife knew what had happened and her comment was, "How are we going to get that thing out of there?" Just as I was about to pull it out, she stopped me. She knew the size of the cotton wad that was inside the little hole. We pulled very slowly and gently and finally got it out. I could imagine trying to explain it to the receptionist in a doctor's office.

The remainder of the trip was uneventful and I got the help I needed. Managing a problem urostomy can be doable. Presently I am able to be active, swim, scuba dive, and spend long hours in the hot tub without making a mess.

Mike Ster is a retired social worker and submarine veteran who learned to dive in the navy in 1951. He is a PADI master instructor and was instrumental in forming the first Underwater Search and Recovery Unit in Cedar Rapids, Iowa. He has been all over the world diving and is a scuba instructor.

Top Five List

Brenda's top five irrigating hints (not so serious).

1. Try to do it alone with no small children in the bathroom with you. (You deserve a break.)
2. Politely refuse the omelet your husband brings to you and offer to have it later— preferably at the breakfast table.
3. When staying in a hotel and the fire alarm goes off as you are irrigating, make sure you have a back-up plan, like a clip.
4. Tell the kids you have to irrigate right when you have the family busy doing the dusting, vacuuming, and laundry.
5. My top irrigating tip? If someone offers to take you out for breakfast right when it is time to irrigate, go. Irrigating can be delayed. Never pass up a free meal.

Tiny Bubbles

I had a bad year in 2004. In the middle of the night, I woke up with severe abdominal pains, which made my abdomen look like I was nine months pregnant. I went to the hospital and remained there for a month while they tried to figure out what to do with me. I dealt with a fistula, blood transfusions, and surgery. They sent me home on TPN (Total Parenteral Nutrition), no food for two months while my insides healed. I was bed ridden for almost seven months. I missed my hula, golf, and exercise, and when I finally began to recover from surgery, I was quite weak. Now, nothing slows me down. I do it all, plus travel and, boy, do I love to eat. I can eat up a storm.

Invited to my brother's fiftieth wedding anniversary celebration, I was in a partying mood after not feeling well for so long. The champagne was flowing. The waiters would fill my glass the moment I turned my back. I wasn't driving, so I didn't care.

I had put on a clean pouch before going, and I felt great. With all the champagne, I could feel gas come in. I had used Hollister's Adapt product in my pouch. When I went to release the gas, the combination of Adapt and champagne made bubbles come out, and I found myself punching them and playing with them. They were clean because there was only gas in my pouch. They were flowing like the bubble machine from the *Lawrence Welk Show*. I have used the Adapt repeatedly and, sadly, no bubbles since that time. I will have to get some more champagne.

Betty Stevens lives in Sun City, California. Blessed with a great extended family along with her own three children, their spouses, and five grandsons, she stays well connected. At the time of her colostomy surgery in 2004, her great-grandchild was just born. They would bring the baby to the hospital, which was great inspiration for Betty to get well. She wanted to hold that precious baby. Other big events, like her daughter's fiftieth birthday party motivated her to get well. Her family rallied around her when things looked tough and having fun plans ahead kept Betty going. She never wants to miss a good time.

Toilet

Items I have dropped into the toilet while irrigating over the last ten years.

Pens

Paper clips

Combs

Jewelry

Perfume (*Is that eau de toilet?*)

Scissors

Books

Deodorant

Note cards

Toothbrush

Magazines

Crossword puzzles

Brush

Q-tips

and just this morning—reading glasses.

Train

There were several people with ostomies at the first international conference held in Denmark for the twenty-to-forty-year-olds. Minnesotan Amy Finley, an ileostomate since 1979 at the age of eighteen, was amongst them. She and a few friends decided to walk to the station to take the train into town. As they were all trying to figure out where and how to purchase their train tickets, they noticed the train was arriving.

As they hurriedly boarded the train, one of the women was slow in getting on. It appeared she was having problems at the doorway. Someone rushed to help her and saw the predicament. Even though the friend had the straps of her purse over her arm, the body of the bag that contained her money, passport, and ticket was stuck in the door, outside of the train.

As they arrived at the next stop, they witnessed the curious looks of the bystanders to the purse hanging midway in the door. Being all ostomates in that car, Amy made the comment, "I can just see the headlines now. *Ostomate gets bag caught in train.*" A group of people were seen laughing heartily as the doors opened to their platform.

Amy Finley, Minnesota native, was diagnosed with ulcerative colitis at age twelve. An ileostomy followed in 1979, but it hasn't stopped her from traveling to Denmark, Canada, and all over the United States. Along the way she has made many friends and helped them to realize that they are not alone and can do things like enjoy soaking in a hot tub or swimming. Amy has been a veterinary tech, done customer service for a medical distributor, and now works for a gastroenterology group as an exit scheduler, setting up appointments for people like herself.

Travelers

The stoma size will change in size the first year after surgery. In the process of changing, leaks can occur because the shape can change from round to an egg shape. While we were at Norris Comprehensive Cancer Hospital, the stoma nurse Cindy looked at Bob's stoma as we expressed our dismay at the amount of leakage from his ostomy. We nicknamed it Mick Jagger because it was so big at first and kept changing into weird shapes like Mick Jagger's mouth.

Cindy, hoping to comfort us said, "Look at that shape, it looks like an eyeball to the soul." Miffed at all the mess we had to clean up, I said, "Cindy, that's not an eyeball to the soul, that's an eyeball to the a—hole." I might have shocked her a little but nothing can distress us anymore. Later, another stoma nurse showed us that by taking your fingers and spreading the egg shape into the round shape and attaching the flange right away, the round shape would eventually return. It worked—and now he has a round stoma.

The first trip by plane after Bob's surgery was to St. Louis, Missouri, to a United Ostomy Association convention. The conference ended and we went to the St. Louis airport to depart for California. Bob was in a wheelchair at that time, and as we came through security, the guard said he would have to use the wand as he was in the wheelchair. After scanning him, he said, "You'll have to take that money belt off." Bob said, "That's not a money belt." "Whatever it is, you'll have to take it off and put it through x-ray." Bob said, "Do you know what an ostomy bag is? That's not a money belt; it is a pouch for poop." They quickly waved him through.

Bob and I met in the Peace Corps forty years ago in Ethiopia. It's amazing to think Bob was not going to make it four years ago with a diagnosis of colorectal cancer and now we have traveled again. We had the good fortune to be in Ethiopia when a delivery of one thousand pounds of ostomy supplies from FOW, Friends of Ostomates Worldwide, arrived. During our visit, we met with dozens of young girls that had urostomies created by fistulas during childbirth. At one of the meetings, many of the young girls were learning to use their ostomy products. Bob shared that he also was an ostomate. Their eyes became extremely wide and their faces very confused because they wondered how a man could have an ostomy since he does not bear children. The Ethiopian stoma therapist translated that there were other kinds of ostomies.

Bob had a colostomy resulting from colorectal cancer. As soon as the girls heard the word cancer, they were amazed that he was alive. Bob was able to share with them that with correct surgery and ostomy equipment, you can lead a life to travel all the way from the USA to come to visit them in Ethiopia.

In December 2004, Oprah Winfrey built a wing of the hospital specifically for these ostomy patients. If they were married, their husbands may cast them out if the baby was dead or because of their constant leakage of urine and body waste.

They would have them stay away in a separate hut and carry food to them because they are shunned from the culture with this defect. On more rare occasions, the family would help get her the correct procedure. When it comes to ostomies, very few people understand ostomy procedures. There is an amazing woman, Dr. Catherine Hamlin, who is the driving force behind correcting this issue for Ethiopian women. She and her husband have done over 50,000 fistula surgeries in this hospital called "The City of Hope." There is a whole book on it called *The Hospital by the River: A Story of Hope* by Dr. Catherine Hamlin with John Little. She tells about the plight of the women and how she came to help them.

Things have a way of working out. Bob had accidents due to his problem with perpetual discharge through the anal area and sometimes it is very bloody. He needs to use Kotex. We call him the Kotex poster boy of the year. Once, in an airport, I saw him have an accident on his beige pants. I quickly got a wheelchair for him and wheeled him to the bathroom. I had extra briefs in our luggage but no other pants. I asked someone nearby if there was a store where I could buy pants, but he couldn't speak English. I found someone else that told me there was nothing available. A woman with an airport office name tag affixed to her jacket heard our inquiries and soon found three different sizes of maintenance workers pants and would take no compensation. While traveling all over the world we have been shown many kindnesses when we least expected it.

Pat Parish is wife of husband, Bob, who had colostomy surgery in 1999. Bob and Pat are still active volunteers with the Peace Corps and worked in 2005 with the evacuees of Hurricane Katrina. They reside in California.

Underneath

I am a reader at the school and read to five classes for twenty minutes at each class. I sit on a chair and the children sit at my feet and are very quiet while they listen. Sometimes I can't help it when the gas comes out and makes a noise. Luckily, it doesn't smell. The children snicker and point at each other, and I stay sober so they never suspect it's me.

My daughter made me a picture made out of photos of our family. One photo in particular made me laugh. I had my tongue sticking out posed next to a bowl of punch, and my granddaughter sat next to me with her hands folded prayer-like. Underneath it was a caption that read, "Come on, Grandma, just one more bowl of Golytely."

Joyce Elza has had a colostomy for twenty years and is a widow and a great-grandmother. She enjoys quilting, sewing, and is active in the local ostomy association.

Undressing

I was in Las Vegas for the United Ostomy conference in 1995, and my buddies and I partied every night in the lounge of the Riviera Hotel. The last night we were there, everybody got wind of it and wanted to join in. A beautiful blonde singer called me up to the stage and, as she sang to me, she started undressing me. I let her of course, and as she took off my shoes and socks, she would throw them one by one out to the crowd. Slowly, she took my shirt off, and then tried to remove my undershirt, but I thought it best to stop her. My friends that were ostomates were laughing hysterically. Eventually, she ended the song, and I had to go through the audience and gather my clothes. We danced and partied all night long.

Larry Trapp of Evansville, Indiana, has been a colostomate since 1988. Larry is the webmaster for the Ostomy Association of Southwestern Indiana's online newsletter. It is packed with useful ostomy information at www.ostomy.evansville.net/contact.

Unexpectedly

There is a health crisis center in Minneapolis called Pathways. They invite people that are in the midst of their health crisis to attend classes free of charge. Alternative therapies such as massage, Reiki, and art therapy were just a few offered to supplement traditional medical care. I participated in a program called Renewing Life when I first dealt with my ostomy.

Rushing to get there on time, I hurried from the bathroom into my bedroom before I put my pouch back on. Unexpectedly, poop went flying all over my bed, my floor, and part of the vanity. There was no way I'd be on time. I was mad at myself and cried as I cleaned up the mess.

When I got to Pathways, they were just about to end their weekly tradition of each person stating their brag and bummer for the week. I told them mine was one in the same. Even though I had just had a painful reminder of having a colostomy,

I put on my prettiest purple dress, fixed my makeup, and went out to face the world.

UPS

I had been dating a man for a little while and the time came when I shared with him that I had gone through ostomy surgery due to Crohn's Disease. You never knew if it would scare the men off. "I used to be sick, and now I am healthy." There were no negative reactions when he heard my details, and he said he wanted to continue seeing me, which pleased me. One night I was over at Chuck's place. The looks and attraction were getting stronger and steamier by the moment between us, and I knew I wanted to go to bed with him. However, I was not at my place where I had all of my ostomy supplies including my little intimate pouch. I said to Chuck, "Do you have any masking tape?" He said quizzically, "Yeah?" He looked funny as I asked him, "Okay, can I have the roll?"

He brought it to me and I told him, "I'll be right back. Stay here and don't go anywhere." I proceeded to go into the bathroom where I rolled up my pouch to make it smaller. Taking the masking tape, I rolled it across from one end to the other and even criss-crossed it to make the pouch stick to my skin. With the help of masking tape, I had a mini pouch raring to go.

I nonchalantly sauntered into the bedroom. With my bra still on, I stood in the doorway and posed, "Hi, I'm your little UPS package and you get to open me up." He burst out laughing; it was a memorable evening.

Lois Fink resides in Washington state and has been living with an ileostomy since 1986, after a nineteen-year battle with Crohn's Disease. Lois enjoys reading, cooking, movies, visiting new places, and fifty percent off "retail therapy." A loyal friend with a wacky sense of humor, she is passionate about causes, especially IBD education. She describes herself as a cross between a boxer and the Energizer bunny.

Used Anus

I am a new ostomy patient and suggested to my surgeon that he might see if he could market my used anus that was removed, you know, like a used car, but he said there is really no market. Having an ostomy isn't something I'd recommend as a weight loss program or how to spend a vacation, but it isn't the end of the world. All my problems have occurred since Bush was elected, so I am blaming him.

Ned Cline is from Greensboro, North Carolina, and has had a colostomy since July 1, 2005. He named his ostomy "Kirk" in honor of his surgeon who did a "World Series" job of putting him back together. Ned spent thirty years as a traveling newspaper reporter/editor, but now teaches, researches, and writes books on worthy philanthropists. He has just finished his fourth book, Pioneers in Faith.

Vesuvius

The classic name for a stoma because of its eruption of bowel contents.

Visit

I was in the hospital for three weeks eating only ice chips while battling ulcerative colitis. Ready for surgery mentally and physically, I was despondent when told it had to be delayed a few days. I am usually positive and up all the time, but this time I cried and it really affected my husband. Surreptitiously, he called the doctor and urged him to change his schedule. Soon after, the surgeon came to my room, knelt down by my bed, put my hands in his, and said he thought he should go ahead and do the surgery the next day. He was so gentle and concerned, and I felt relieved to be finally getting it done.

On the day I was scheduled for surgery for an ileostomy a nurse said to me, " I would rather be dead than have ostomy surgery." I don't think her timing was great, but she was being honest.

After I had my surgery, and the NG tube came out, we were waiting for signs of bowel activity. An awesome nurse worked with me and got very excited when she saw green smelly stuff coming out onto my skin. "This is normal, that's what it's supposed to do." She was joyful and made me feel good about it. After she cleaned me up, she put on the urostomy pouch. The hospital didn't have an ET on staff yet; she wouldn't arrive for two more weeks. My nurse might not have known what was the right equipment, but she had the right attitude. During my hospital stay, I had visits from another nurse with a urostomy and an anesthesiologist who had a urostomy, both had heard about me and wanted to assure me that all would be well. Later, I had a visit from a very attractive young woman wearing a white pleated skirt with hair piled up on her head, and she told me she had a baby too. Her five-minute visit helped me to see I would be okay.

I have never had a down day. It probably isn't normal, but I have a good family that supports me, and it wasn't until ten years later that I learned how sick I really was and that my husband had asked the surgeon to reconsider his schedule.

I went on to have a second child, and he'll be twenty-three soon. The nurse with the ostomy went on to become an ET and she and the anesthesiologist that visited me became friends and stayed involved with our local ostomy chapter.

Ginnie Kasten and her husband, John, of thirty-two years have two grown children and live in Illinois. She has worked as a schoolteacher and now works for an attorney in family law. She is currently the secretary of the new UOAA and has been involved with her local chapter for twenty-five years. She loves music and likes to sing in her church choir.

Wand

I was going through the airport security in San Diego when I set off the alarm. They took the wand up, down, and came across my pouch and set off another alarm. I explained to them what it was. The security guard said, "I am sorry we have to check it out." They took me into a private room and told me to take my pants down. The younger security guard said, "My uncle's got one of those. You're okay to go ahead." I complimented them because they handled it well, and now I take off anything that has potential to set off alarms.

Brian Bowden and his wife reside in California. A year after Brian retired from a thirty-year career with the United Way, he found he had cancer. He lost a total year in productivity, but earned a year of reflection when his busy life stopped. He appreciated the family and friends that surrounded him and the power of prayer he had long forgotten. When first diagnosed, he researched the Internet and contacted the American Cancer Society who connected him to the United Ostomy Association. Within a short time, he was visiting about his upcoming surgery with another man who had a urostomy. Brian promotes the ostomy visitor model because of the comfort he felt facing surgery. He keeps busy consulting for non-profits and is the current president for his local ostomy chapter.

Wardrobe Malfunction

We live in Wisconsin where it is very agricultural. When I was younger, my father took me to the University of Madison to see a unique live cow. This cow on campus had a window in it where you could see one of its stomachs and the inner workings of its digestive tract. Now I have one too, which is where it got the nickname of "my little science project." It was going to be temporary while we saw how it worked—which eventually became permanent.

I was at the United Ostomy Association conference in California talking to a bunch of young adults, and we ended up talking about when accidents happen with the pouches. As we shared stories, I said, "About 95 percent of the time you have an accident because you're being lazy or doing something stupid like living on borrowed time with your pouch. Usually you know when you should do it, but then you're running late in the morning and that's when you get into trouble, thinking you can stretch it out one more day. Just then, we got up to get ice cream, and I had my own version of a "wardrobe malfunction," a massive leak on my shirt and shorts. I had to laugh at myself. There were other reasons a person could have an accident. I had been to the stoma clinic less than twenty-four hours before and tried new products that the nurse recommended. I won't be using that one again.

John Blotz of Wisconsin is a thirty-five-year-old, five-year ileosto-mate, married with children. He enjoys spending time with his family and on the job sites as a construction manager. He jokes that he gets to use many port-o-potties. He enjoys doing home improvements, music, and is a shade tree mechanic.

Winnie the Pooh-er

The Monday before Thanksgiving, I had surgery to remove a tumor found in my colon. They removed approximately eighteen inches of colon, re-sectioned it, and sewed me back up. I told the doctor that I was giving him a chance to practice his carving before he got to the turkey.

It turned out the cancer had spread. I had a spot on my liver, bladder, in my lung, and some on the walls of the abdomen. When I talked with the oncologist, I asked him what I was looking at. He replied, "By the book, you have eighteen months." I informed him, "I've never done anything by the book, and I'm not starting now." I was true to my word, which was three years ago.

In February 2004, we started looking at the possibility of a colostomy. By December, I was having so many problems, I decided I was going to have a Merry Christmas and a Happy New "Rear." With this type of surgery, I would still have my rectum. This prevented me from having the doctor report to my family that, "The operation was a success—there's no end in sight." I ended up with a colostomy, which I call Winnie the Pooh-er.

I was awake and watching when he opened the loop to create the stoma. He used a cauterizing tool to open it. I remarked, "I am going to have to start calling you Moses." When he asked why, I responded, "Because it looks like you're parting the Red Sea." It has taken some getting used to, but I am doing better now. I am still charging on with the chemo and tolerating it fairly well. It sure beats the alternative.

John Woodfin, forty-eight years old from Alabama, is a cancer fighter. John spent twenty-one years working inside a prison as a correctional officer. He has a passion for hunting, traveling, and his wife of almost twenty-two years, Nancy. They have three grown sons, along with their wives, and are about to have their sixth grandchild.

Wiped

October 24, 1995. The last time the author of this book wiped her butt.

Women

Grown women can actually get almost completely out of control when they get together. In our forties, the three of us only

discovered each other a few years ago, yet we relate as if its been a lifetime. We spent a luxurious Mom's weekend away from kids and spouses, ate what and when we wanted, and went to bed several times a day or night. Nestled in a cabin in the woods of northern Minnesota overlooking a beautiful lake, our biggest decisions were about snacking or beverages. We did the usual things during the day—fishing, eating, reading, and enjoyed the solitary hours as well as the together time.

We discussed our bathroom habits, and how I would need the only bathroom available for an hour in the morning. Women in their forties have strong urges when waking so I wanted to make sure their needs were met for the bathroom too. We had adjusted to my routine, and that discussion was behind us. Conversations erupted unceasingly like lava tumbling out of a volcano. No subject was off limits, and we guffawed so hard I thought my neck would explode.

Laughter flowed as we taunted our dear friend Renee about her choice of pajamas. "Do they squelch all possible passion from your husband?" In good humor, we put her on the hot seat, her face getting redder under the scrutinizing lights of our never-ending questions. Clearly, we had broke the barrier of remaining polite and proper with each other when she teasingly yelled, "Okay, Brenda, if you don't quit this torture, I'm going to grab you by your stoma and wrap it around your neck until you stop." Bladders weak already from the hours of chortling, we almost wet our pants at her outburst. I have never heard of anyone threatening to pull a stoma before.

"Officer, I would like to press charges on my friend Renee Rongen."

"Why's that Ma'am?"

"Sir, she's threatened my stoma!"

"Oh, yes, penal code 78.35 states any threat of stoma pull requires the offender to subject themselves to a full colonoscopy without medication." I laughed so hard I could hardly breathe. Amongst our wild fun and seriously warped humor, I knew this friendship was sealed in love and acceptance.

Wonderful

What could be wonderful about having your rectum removed? My brother would be able tell you; he has an answer for almost everything. "No skid marks on your underwear."

Wrestling

I was wrestling with my niece and nephew, and we were tickling each other and one of them ended up behind me on the couch with his face at my behind. One of my family members made the familiar comment, "You better hope she doesn't let one go right now." I said, "That would be impossible from back there." It stopped conversation for a second before everyone burst out laughing with the realization there was no danger of that happening.

X

X-ray

I went down to the x-ray department, and they were going to do a barium enema. At the time, I still had a colostomy because of ulcerative colitis. As I lay almost completely naked on the table, the nurse assistant put the barium drip on the dead side of my intestines. Because it was constricted, the barium explosively flew back out all over me, all over the nurse, all over the equipment, and all over the doctor. The nurse assistant profusely apologized while she handed me one pathetic piece of tissue as the barium ran down over my breast and through my legs. The nurse was so uncomfortable that she ran out of the room. I said to the doctor, "After this, nothing could embarrass me again." Everybody laughed and it broke the tension.

Susan Burns, of St. Peters, Missouri, had a colostomy for three months before getting an ileostomy in 1989. She is married with two children and two grandchildren and likes needlepoint and traveling. She works part time as a beauty consultant at Kohl's department store and is an independent contractor for the St. Louis Convention and Visitors Commission.

Yard Work

My neighbors' kids were out helping us do yard work one day, and they came across a huge poop that looked too big to have come from our mid-size dog. They were wondering where it came from, and I looked at them and their parents and said, "Don't look at me!"

Anita Singewald, ileostomate from Minnesota.

Youth Rally

I was on the national board of directors for the United Ostomy Association and was invited to go to San Jose, California, for the Youth Rally. I met several other counselors, then learned about the kids and the different surgeries they had endured. One day we planned an excursion to the Paramount Theme Park up in Costa Mesa. That morning we had rap sessions with the youth and ate our lunch on the San Jose State campus where we stayed. Then we walked several blocks to downtown San Jose to catch the light rail to the park.

In 1990, after twenty-five years of ulcerative colitis, I had ileostomy surgery. I felt comfortable with my ostomy and happy to be participating in the rally. The kids are amazing, and the counselors are dedicated to making the kids have the best fun possible despite the many social and emotional issues related to individual situations.

As we walked to the rail station, I noticed a familiar odor and to my horror, when I looked down at my feet, there was my bag *and* wafer! My ostomy was active and stuff was running down my leg and staining my pants. I felt frustrated, told a couple of the ET nurses what was happening, and started to look for a restroom. Our backpacks had plenty of paper towels and extra supplies, but there was no time as the light rail train had arrived. In that moment, I weighed out going back to the dorms where I'd remain alone all day or continue on with the kids to the park. I put paper towels around my stoma and headed to the park.

When we arrived, we went through security and then went to the place for the kids and counselors to use as a base. Kids were allowed to roam the park alone or with friends. For many, it was their first taste of independence. Everyone was wearing their Youth Rally t-shirts so we could spot each other anywhere in the park. I had stained my shirt so I went to buy a replacement, then proceeded to the restrooms to clean up. I spent an hour cleaning myself the best I could using paper towels and toilet water. It was not easy and took a long time, but at last I had a new wafer and bag on.

I was angry about the whole incident. How was I going to show a positive face to the kids? Several of the counselors had learned of my accident and offered support. Many of the kids asked where I had disappeared to, and, when I told them what had happened, they offered their comforting sentiments. A role reversal had occurred. They shared their own stories about similar incidents, and we were able to find humor in the situation. It also showed them that even adults have accidents and it was not the end of the world. After more kids found out, some of them would give me a pat on the back, or a hug, and go on with their day. I was impressed that these kids had so much compassion for me. They taught me a lesson that day.

Steve Strizic was diagnosed with ulcerative colitis at age seventeen and had an ileostomy in 1990. Single and living in Tacoma, Washington, he likes to travel and make new friends.

Zebra

In the early hours of a Saturday morning, Nancy had emergency abdominal surgery with a temporary colostomy placement. She had spent five days and nights in the surgical ICU due to low blood pressure and several other issues. Transferred to the surgical floor, she slept fitfully around the clock.

Nancy had an NG tube, urinary catheter, and several IV lines dripping with antibiotics and other unpronounceable medicines. She had been given pain medicines for obvious reasons, was tossing and turning, and only opening her eyes to see if I was still in the darkened room. I sat in a chair to her right, reading a dog-eared magazine for the twenty-third time, and the wall-mounted TV was on to provide distraction and ambient noise.

The TV show of the moment was an animal safari program, complete with lions chasing prey so they could feed their cubs. There were antelopes, cheetahs, and others maintaining the status quo of the animal kingdom. I hadn't even noticed the TV until Nancy said, "James, if there was a merciful God—He would have put vertical stripes on that zebra's butt."

When we came home from the hospital, we faced an unexpected event. We were learning how to maintain a colostomy and our sense of humor and found it to be a challenge at times. Nancy was lying in the bed, still not even wanting to look at her colostomy. I am a registered nurse with years of emergency room practice, but I had little experience dealing with the ostomy. While I was performing routine care and the bag was detached, Nancy's intestines became active, and we were both at a loss what to do. Nancy was mortified. She has always been a private person, and this situation was almost too much to bear. I pulled from my nursing experience and dealt with the issue at hand, but the embarrassment consumed Nancy. I tried to console her while I worked.

She looked at me through tears and told me repeatedly how much she appreciated my willingness to care for her during this ordeal. I told her how much I loved her and how I knew if our roles were reversed, she would take care of me the same way.

Still crying, she looked up at me and said, "No, but I would pay someone to."

James Hammons was in the Navy and traveled the world before he decided to become an ER nurse and, for fun, a part time musician in a beach music band. He was a major caretaker of his fiancée, Nancy Hall, who has loved him since she was fourteen years old.

To Conclude

I n 2005, the national office of the United Ostomy Association was dissolved. Part of the reason was that there was low membership. In North America, there are 700,000 ostomates, and yet the enrolled members of the United Ostomy Association numbered about 22,000. Judging from many of these stories, the benefits of that organization were profound. In addition, the numbers may not reveal how many people had joined, and then not renewed their membership when they received all they needed from the support aspect of the program. Organized visitor programs, newsletters, and monthly meetings with topics relevant to the ostomate were, and continue to be, a very successful facet of many of the chapters in existence today. Many more people seek information from the Internet or get what they need directly from their surgeons who may have set up a support system in their local hospital or clinic.

When I walked into my first meeting, I saw normal looking people standing around, smiling, and joking. They looked confident and attractive and were enjoying each other. I was blown away. Subconsciously, I must have expected people to be standing around looking morose and awkwardly shy. Perhaps my feelings inside were being projected into my thoughts. At first, I wondered if I was at the wrong place. These people were having too much fun. Up to this moment, I was the only one I knew with an ostomy.

Suddenly, I wasn't a big deal anymore. My problems weren't outrageous and horrific; they were commonplace amongst this group. I was not special or unique anymore with my problem. I had a major shift at that first meeting. Time to move on with life. Quit putting off desires or goals and don't let the ostomy be my excuse.

The people there acknowledged me and listened as I asked questions. They offered ideas and then moved on. It was all so ordinary that it took a while to sink in. I have to deal with my ostomy every day, but it would not dictate my life.

It's natural to feel badly about having ostomy surgery, and it deserves some time for grief, to pause, to feel the loss of body parts and to adjust. Soon enough, we will have to deal with the demands in the office, the garden club, or driving our kids to soccer. We do the best each day to look at things with a positive spin instead of with a sense of doom. I came to realize there were far worse things in life than dealing with an ostomy.

While preparing this book, I continued this project in California, interviewing fifty ostomates over a three-day period. They helped me to understand the larger experience than my own narrow perspective of dealing with an ostomy as a result of cancer. As the emails and personal interviews continued over the year, my comprehension became even broader, and I am grateful for that knowledge. I noticed the impact the former United Ostomy Association had on a great many contributors, inspiring many to take on leadership roles and to volunteer time with their local chapters.

Many stories were about accidents involving clips, and I liked learning about how inventive others could be with last minute solutions to their dilemmas. I hope those contributors have had a chance to try the latest technology that doesn't require using a clip. To stay current with the newest options, it is important to sign up for free newsletters, the new *Phoenix Magazine*, and attend appliance fairs in your region. More than ever before, the Internet is the source for the latest information and there are chat rooms to talk with other people living with ostomies from all over the world. Go to a meeting if there is one in your area. There is a language spoken there of understanding and encouragement to move forward that comes along with a smile. Many chapters have visitor programs set up to visit new ostomates in the hospital.

For most of us, ostomy surgery was a lifesaver. Our partners are happier because our quality of life might be better than it has been for a long time. Our energy levels might be pushing us to try new things we had long given up on. Not too long ago, my cousin Kelli told me that her client was talking about her grandmother needing to have a colostomy and how horrified her young client was of the whole idea. She relayed that her grandmother was particularly upset that the doctor told her that she had only two choices—get the colostomy or die. Indignantly, the granddaughter said to Kelli, "No one will ever make that choice for me. I would rather die than have a bag of poop hanging off of my body the rest of my life." Then Kelli told her client, who was a young mother, about me. She told her about how my children had been three and five years old when I was diagnosed with cancer of the rectum. About how I owned a business and was happily married and about how many friends and family would have missed me. She asked her client, "Would you have given up all that if you had been told you had to have a colostomy?" "I guess not," her client said quietly.

Many of us have experienced this kind of reaction to the possibility of living with an ostomy. Perhaps you had similar thoughts that you would rather die than have this surgery. Education in this area is crucial, and I thank all the people that submitted stories for the glimpse into your lives. Just as my cousin observed my daily living with an ostomy, we inadvertently educate one person at a time that this situation is livable and a healthy alternative.

I set out to write this book hoping to show that ostomates, and the people that care for them, can have a sense of humor about something serious. I thought other people would have stories, as I did, that were funny and would like to share with others. It broadened to include a slice of life in everyday anecdotes and some inspiration too. From nurses who passionately shared a love of their career choice and their patients to care givers and family members who helped in endless ways, I have been touched by each story.

I started realizing how little I knew about the struggles of so many, especially those that had battled IBD. Since talking to over one hundred people involved with this book, I have found myself saying that I was grateful for only having had four life threatening major surgeries with colorectal cancer and not some of these horrific bowel diseases. It has been said that we wouldn't trade problems with another. Maybe that's true. As I talked to others that had read my first book, they felt grateful they just had ulcerative colitis or Crohn's Disease. I think we learn to cope somehow with whatever comes our way. Some people do it with humor. Others remain private while some make the decision to go full disclosure as my husband and I. It is a personal family decision. What you decide to make public can affect the whole family. Luckily for us, it has been very positive. We have been able to open the doors of discussion for what many still consider a taboo subject. We have no regrets, and to give up our privacy about this issue has not hurt us in any way. Instead, it has empowered us and made us feel good for sharing important private information that we hope only helps others.

This became a collective project of many voices of experience and humor. I thank all those new friends for their stories; I am proud to be amongst you. I have learned that an ostomy may be the very thing that brings out a passion you didn't know you had, and, instead, can make you thrive in the world in a way you never imagined. For many of us, we get to see the world and be a part of it. There's no holding us back!

What's Your Story?

To all nurses, people living with ostomies, or loved ones and caretakers: If you have a funny or inspirational true unpublished story you would like to submit for future publication, please send it to me, along with your contact information. Story submissions will require your permission to be used. There will be no monetary compensation for stories nor any guarantee of using submitted stories. Your comments and suggestions for this or future publications or newsletters are welcomed and encouraged.

Appendix A

The Role of the Intestine

To understand the role of the intestine, let us follow the path that food takes as it passes through and is digested by the body. Food first enters the body through the mouth, where it is cut into small pieces by the teeth and broken down somewhat by the saliva. The food is then swallowed and passes to the stomach down a long tube called the esophagus. Stomach muscles and gastric juices act on the food to further break it down and prepare it for absorption by the blood. After several hours the pulpy mass of food passes into the small intestine, a twenty-foot long tube that is folded and packed into the abdominal cavity.

This small intestine–named not for its length, but for the narrow diameter is where most digestion takes place. At the end of its processing, all that remains is water and waste material, which then passes into the large intestine, or colon. This portion of the intestine is about five feet long and has a much larger diameter (thus, its name, large intestine). The colon's function is to absorb the water from the waste material, to transport waste through its length, and to store it until it is ready to be expelled from the body through the anus.

Used with permission from Hollister Incorporated

Appendix B

What is Crohn's Disease?

Crohn's Disease is a chronic (ongoing) disorder that causes inflammation of the digestive or gastrointestinal (GI) tract. Although it can involve any area of the GI tract from the mouth to the anus, it most commonly affects the small intestine and/or colon.

The disease is named after Dr. Burrill B. Crohn. In 1932, Dr. Crohn and two colleagues, Dr. Leon Ginzburg and Dr. Gordon D. Oppenheimer, published a landmark paper describing the features of what is known today as Crohn's Disease. Crohn's and a related disease, ulcerative colitis, are the two main disease categories that belong to a larger group of illnesses called inflammatory bowel disease (IBD).

Because the symptoms of these two illnesses are so similar, it is sometimes difficult to establish the diagnosis definitively. In fact, approximately 10 percent of colitis cases are unable to be pinpointed as either ulcerative colitis or Crohn's Disease and are called indeterminate colitis.

Although Crohn's Disease most commonly affects the end of the small intestine (the ileum) and the beginning of the large intestine (the colon), it may involve any part of the GI tract. In ulcerative colitis, on the other hand, the GI involvement is limited to the colon. In Crohn's Disease, all layers of the intestine may be involved, and there can be normal healthy bowel in between patches of diseased bowel. In contrast, ulcerative colitis affects only the superficial layers (the mucosa) of the colon in a more even and continuous distribution, which starts at the level of the anus.

What Causes Crohn's Disease and Ulcerative Colitis?

Although considerable progress has been made in IBD research, investigators do not yet know what causes this disease. Studies indicate that the inflammation in IBD involves a complex interaction of factors: the genes the person has inherited, the immune system, and something in the environment. Foreign substances (antigens) in the environment may be the direct cause of the inflammation, or they may stimulate the body's defenses to produce an inflammation that continues without control. Researchers believe that once the IBD patient's immune system is "turned on," it does not know how to properly "turn off" at the right time. As a result, inflammation damages the intestine and causes the symptoms of IBD. That is why the main goal of medical therapy is to help patients regulate their immune system better.

How Common is Inflammatory Bowel Disease (IBD)?

It is estimated that as many as one million Americans have IBD—with that number evenly split between Crohn's Disease and ulcerative colitis. Males and females appear to be affected equally. Crohn's Disease may occur in people of all ages, but it is primarily a disease of adolescents and young adults, affecting mainly those between fifteen and thirty-five. However, Crohn's Disease can also occur in people who are seventy or older and in young children as well. In fact, 10 percent of those affected-or an estimated 100,000-are youngsters under the age of eighteen.

Who Gets IBD?

IBD tends to run in families, so we know that genes definitely play a role in the IBD picture. Studies have shown that about 20 to 25 percent of patients may have a close relative with either Crohn's or ulcerative colitis. If a person has a relative with the disease, his or her risk is about ten times greater than that of the general population. If that relative happens to be a brother or sister, the risk is thirty times greater.

Persistent diarrhea (loose, watery, or frequent bowel movements), crampy abdominal pain, fever, and, at times, rectal bleeding: These are the hallmark symptoms of Crohn's Disease, but they vary from person to person and may change over time. Loss of appetite and subsequent weight loss also may occur. However, the disease is not always limited to the GI tract; it can also affect the joints, eyes, skin, and liver. Fatigue is another common complaint. Children who have Crohn's Disease may suffer delayed growth and sexual development.

Some patients may develop tears (fissures) in the lining of the anus, which may cause pain and bleeding, especially during bowel movements. Inflammation may also cause a fistula to develop. A fistula is a tunnel that leads from one loop of intestine to another, or that connects the intestine to the bladder, vagina, or skin. Fistulas occur most commonly around the anal area. If this complication arises, you may notice drainage of mucus, pus, or stool from this opening.

Symptoms may range from mild to severe. Because Crohn's is a chronic disease, patients will go through periods in which the disease flares up, is active, and causes symptoms. These episodes are followed by times of remission-periods in which symptoms disappear or decrease and good health returns. In general, though, people with Crohn's Disease lead full, active, and productive lives.

What is Ulcerative Colitis?

Ulcerative colitis is a chronic (ongoing) disease of the colon, or large intestine. The disease is marked by inflammation and ulceration of the colon mucosa, or innermost lining. Tiny open sores, or ulcers, form on the surface of the lining, where they bleed and produce pus and mucus. Because the inflammation makes the colon empty frequently, symptoms typically include diarrhea (sometimes bloody) and often crampy abdominal pain.

The inflammation usually begins in the rectum and lower colon, but it may also involve the entire colon. When ulcerative colitis affects only the lowest part of the colon—the rectum—it is called ulcerative proctitis. If the disease affects only the left side of the colon, it is called limited or distal colitis. If it involves the entire colon, it is termed pancolitis.

Neither ulcerative colitis nor Crohn's Disease should be confused with irritable bowel syndrome (IBS), a disorder that affects the motility (muscle contractions) of the colon. Sometimes called "spastic colon" or "nervous colitis," IBS is not characterized by intestinal inflammation. It is, therefore, a much less serious disease than ulcerative colitis. IBS bears no direct relationship to either ulcerative colitis or Crohn's Disease.

CCFA-sponsored research has led to progress in the fields of immunology, the study of the body's immune defense system; microbiology, the study of microscopic organisms with the power to cause disease; and genetics. Many scientists now believe that the interaction of an outside agent (such as a virus or bacterium) with the body's immune system may trigger the disease, or that such an agent may cause damage to the intestinal wall, initiating or accelerating the disease process. Through CCFA's continuing research efforts, much more will be learned and a cure will eventually be found.

Used with permission by CCFA, Crohn's and Colitis Foundation of America

Appendix C

Colorectal Cancer

Colorectal cancer is one of the reasons people end up with an ostomy. Colorectal cancer is one of the leading causes of cancer deaths among both men and women in the United States today, yet it is the most preventable and treatable cancer if caught early enough. A colonoscopy or sigmoidoscopy procedure may reveal evidence of cancer. A fecal occult blood test (FOBT) may detect small amounts of blood in the stool and ideally should be used in conjunction with a colonoscopy or sigmoidoscopy. A blood count may reveal evidence of anemia with low iron levels.

Most early cases of colon cancer have no symptoms. If there is a history of colon cancer in the family, it is recommended each member be evaluated ten years before the age of that person diagnosed. For example, I was diagnosed at age thirty-nine, then all my siblings at age twenty-nine and older should be tested immediately. In my family of ten, at least four members had precancerous polyps removed. The following symptoms, however, may indicate colon cancer:

- Diarrhea, constipation, or other change in bowel habits
- Blood in the stool or bleeding from the rectum
- Unexplained anemia

- Abdominal pain and tenderness in the lower abdomen
- Cramping
- Intestinal obstruction
- Decreased appetite or weight loss with no known reason
- Stools narrower than usual
- Weakness and fatigue
- Jaundice (yellow-green color of the skin and white part of the eye)

Appendix D

The Various Types of Ostomies

Not all ostomies are the same.

A colostomy is a surgically created opening into the colon through the abdomen. Its purpose is to allow the stool to bypass a diseased or damaged part of the colon. A colostomy may be made at almost any point along the length of the colon. When you have a colostomy, stool is no longer eliminated though the anus.

Instead, it is eliminated through the colostomy. To construct a colostomy, the surgeon brings part of the colon through the abdominal wall. This new opening on the abdomen is called a stoma. An ileostomy is a surgically created opening into the small intestine through the abdomen. The purpose of an ileostomy is to allow stool to bypass the colon.

Because of an injury or disease, such as ulcerative colitis or Crohn's Disease, the colon may be surgically removed, along with the rectum and anus. Remember, the colon's main purpose is to absorb water and store stool. Your body can continue to function even without a colon.

When you have an ileostomy, stool is no longer eliminated through the anus. Instead, stool is eliminated through the ileostomy. An ileostomy, like the colostomy, does not have a sphincter muscle, so you have no voluntary control over bowel movements. Instead, you will wear a disposable pouch to collect the stool. An ileostomy, like the colostomy, may be temporary or permanent, depending on the medical reason for the surgery.

A urostomy is a surgically created opening usually on the abdomen. A urostomy allows urine to flow out of the body after the bladder has been removed or bypassed. A urostomy may also be called a urinary diversion. When a person has a urostomy, urine is no longer eliminated through the urethra. Instead, it is eliminated through the urostomy. Because a urostomy does not have a sphincter muscle, you have no voluntary control over when to urinate. Instead, you wear a pouch to collect the urine.

Used with permission from Hollister Incorporated

Options

When a patient needs to undergo removal of their entire large intestine (the colon and rectum) a new pathway for the evacuation of digestive waste will be necessary. There are surgical options for patients who need to undergo total colectomy. All options are available for patients with both UC (Ulcerative Colitis) and FAP (Familial Adenomatous Polyposis).

Ileoanal "J" Pouch

The operation that has been performed since the early 1980s involves removing the colon and upper rectum but leaving the anal canal. An internal pouch is created from the small intestine, and this is connected to the anal canal. This operation goes by many names including J-pouch, ileoanal pouch, the pull-through procedure, and the IPAA (ileal pouch-anal anastomosis).

Modified Kock Pouch-Continent Ileostomy

This operation was devised by Dr. Nils Kock in Sweden in 1969. It involves removing the colon and rectum and anal canal in the traditional way. At that point a pouch is created from the patient's own small intestine together with an intestinal valve. This is not a foreign device or object of any kind but is a doubled layer of small intestine. It is then brought as a stoma through the abdominal wall. Several times a day the person will insert a tube (catheter) into the opening into the pouch and evacuate their intestinal waste into the toilet. There is no pain associated with this and there is no protruding stoma. The intestinal valve creates a self-sealing pouch so that no stool or gas will escape in between draining it. In addition, water from swimming or diving cannot enter the pouch.

Used with Permission from The Quality Life Association, Inc.

All the information above is useful in beginning the important discussions between you and your experienced gastroenterologist, WOCN, and colorectal surgeon. It is also helpful to write down questions or concerns in advance of your appointments so you are prepared when you meet your health professionals.

Appendix E

Informational Websites

- American Cancer Society, www.cancer.org
- The American Society of Colon and Rectal Surgeons, www.fascrs.org
- Association for the Bladder Exstrophy Community, www.bladderexstrophy.com
- Brenda Elsagher, www.livingandlaughing.com
- CCFA (Crohn's & Colitis Foundation of America), www.ccfa.org
- Colon Cancer Alliance, www.ccalliance.org
- The Colon Club, www.colonclub.com
- The Fistula Foundation, www.fistulafoundation.org
- FOW (Friends of Ostomates Worldwide), www.fowusa.org
- GYGIG (Get Your Guts In Gear), www.ibdride.org
- Hollister Incorporated, www.hollister.com
- International Ostomy Association, www.ostomyinternational.org
- The J-Pouch Group, www.j-pouch.org
- National Cancer Institute, www.cancer.gov

- National Colon Cancer Alliance, www.nccra.org
- National Institutes of Health, www.nih.gov
- Pathways Health Crisis Resource Center, www.pathwaysminneapolis.org
- Quality Life Association, www.qla-ostomy.org
- The Phoenix, The Official Publication of UOAA, www.uoaa.org
- Secure Start Newsletter, www.hollister.com
- United Ostomy Association of America, Inc., www.uoaa.org
- United Ostomy Association of Canada, Inc., www.ostomycanada.ca
- Wound, Ostomy, and Continence Nurses Society, www.wocn.org

About the Author

Brenda Elsagher lives in Burnsville, Minnesota, with her husband, Bahgat, her two teenagers, John and Jehan, and their dog, Abby. Brenda is a national keynote speaker, a regular columnist for Hollister's Secure Start Newsletter, and soon able to join AARP and the Red Hat society. She likes to read, cook, strum on her Celtic harp (ever hopeful of making a recognizable tune), write, laugh with her family, nap, play scrabble, eat a good meal with a few friends, watch movies, and recumbent bike, and not particularly in that order.

She is available for speaking engagements and would love to come to your area. Brenda is able to provide an accredited talk for the medical field.

You can contact her at www.livingandlaughing.com.

If you would like to order additional copies of this book, please go to my website at www.livingandlaughing.com or call me at 952-882-0154. I also like to receive questions for my column in the Secure Start Newsletter sent out by Hollister Incorporated. Subscribe today; it's free!